Crooked River Rats

THE ADVENTURES OF PIONEER RIVERMEN

by Bernard McKay

Illustrated by Wendy Liddle

hancock

house

ISBN 0-88839-451-9
Copyright © 2000 Bernard McKay

Cataloging in Publication Data
McKay, Bernard.
  Crooked river rats

  ISBN 0-88839-451-9

  1. Inland water transportation—British Columbia, Northern—
History. 2. Boatmen—British Columbia, Northern—Biography.
I. Title.
HE635.Z7B75 1999   386'.3'097118   C99-910595-7

We acknowledge the financial support of the Government of Canada through the
Book Publishing Industry Development Program for our publishing activities.

We acknowledge the assistance of the Province of British Columbia, through the
British Columbia Arts Council.

Editor: Nancy Miller
Production: Ingrid Luters and Nancy Miller
Cover design: Ingrid Luters
Cover photograph: Don Adams

Published simultaneously in Canada and the United States by

HANCOCK HOUSE PUBLISHERS LTD.
19313 Zero Avenue, Surrey, B.C. V4P 1M7
(604) 538-1114 Fax (604) 538-2262

HANCOCK HOUSE PUBLISHERS
1431 Harrison Avenue, Blaine, WA 98230-5005
(604) 538-1114 Fax (604) 538-2262
Web Site: www.hancockhouse.com *email:* sales@hancockhouse.com

Contents

wendyliode, cci

Acknowledgments

I sometimes think I was born thirty years too late and missed most of the action. I was only twenty-four years old, newly married and living in Prince George, B.C., when the glory days of the rivermen were ending forever in 1972. The keen interest I now have in riverboating was honed listening to the old-timers reminisce about life on the Finlay, Crooked and Parsnip Rivers before development and dams.

To compile this book, I traveled north to Hudson Hope in the Peace River area of B.C. and south to Victoria with stops in between for hundreds of hours of interviews with the people who lived in the river country of the Rocky Mountain Trench. In the process of writing this book it has been a thrill for me to meet more of the old-timers, although there are not many of them left. I regret to say that some of them have passed on between the time I interviewed them and the time this book came into print. I have been privileged to know them and am grateful for their stories. Their descendants and relatives have kept old photos and stories and they have been a big help in putting this book together. To them, I give my most heartfelt thanks.

Among those I spoke with included: Bob Beattie, Sheilah Bebo, Edith Bell, Frank and Connie Buchanan, Harry Chingee, Jack Corless, Joan Curtin, Walter Gill, Edith Hennig, Dave Kylo, Ken Kylo, Jack Little, Steve Marynovich, Fr. Ivan McCormick, Jack Milburn, Jim Miller, Margaret Moore, Carl and Emily New, George and Marjory New, Tom Ole, Len Pickering, Pen Powel, Frank Roberts, Clyde Smaaslett, Ken Stanyer, Andy Stetner, Lorne Swanell, Bill Van Somer, Jim and Louise Van Somer, Milt Warren, Norman and Viola Weatherly, Oliver Williams, Jerry Witter, and Art and Gwanda Yeulet.

I am deeply indebted to the people noted above who graciously allowed me to copy and share their treasured photographs. I would like to thank them again.

Organizations that assisted me included the Prince George Public Library, Prince George Museum, Mackenzie Museum, Hudson Hope Museum, the Prince George Catholic Church Diocese, and the Oblate Archives in Vancouver. Thank you to you all.

The keen memories of Don Adams, Frank Buchanan, George New and Carl New filled in a lot of previously blank history for me. Ken Christopher (the stepson of Ben Corke) has retained a lot of comical details of his stepfather and other people that he knew personally while he was being raised on the Finlay River at Red Ruby Creek.

Special thanks are reserved for Al Huble and Jim Van Somer. This book would not have been possible without their help.

I'm grateful to Wendy Liddle who, as usual, did an excellent job with her sketches. Wendy has done the drawings for both of my books and is a founding member of Cowboy Cartoonists International.

My high school English has gone down hill sadly these thirty-three years out of school and I want to thank my neighbor and hunting partner Warren Eastland for helping me straighten out my convoluted sentences, fractured phrases and laughable spelling. Warren is a master with the English language and a whiz on the computer. Thanks also to Dan Brown for the proofreading.

Finally, I want to thank my wife Jo-Eane who managed to decipher my longhand chicken scratch well enough to type out the stories. She occasionally accompanied me for the interviews and helped with the editing.

Deserters Canyon, 1958.

Photo: Bill Van Somer

Introduction

Today as motorists travel the John Hart Highway running north from Prince George they will see the Crooked River appear on the west side of the road. It is a very slow-running stream that is for the most part shallow and often very narrow. Yes, the river is unimposing and quiet now, but only fifty years ago this river was the only highway to the north and, as such, teemed with activity. All the freight to the north was carried along the Crooked, Pack, Parsnip, Finlay and Peace Rivers by long riverboat. The decades of the 1920s, 1930s and 1940s were the heyday of the rivermen. These were the years when the price of wild fur was high. Roads had penetrated the headwaters of the Crooked and Pack Rivers by the 1950s, but the country northward still was serviced mainly by riverboats until 1969 when Williston Lake was formed by hydro development, thereby cutting off the rivers.

The communities and trading posts of McLeod Lake, Finlay Forks, Fort Graham and Fort Ware all depended on the river highways for their existence. Generations of trappers, hunters and big game guides, as well as independent prospectors depended on the boats for their supplies. These provisions would, in many cases, have to last an entire winter; freight being almost impossible to move during the November to April freeze up.

The book begins with events that took place before the advent of motorized power, when river travel required simple, brute strength. I then continued with stories that took place through the 1920s and 1930s when outboard engines arrived on the scene. Trappers and the trapping industry are what opened up all of Canada and this book would be remiss if these enterprising men were not given their due. I have included discussions on what life was like for the men and women who braved the rivers and the hardships of northern wilderness life. To this end, I have included excerpts from letters and diaries of the day that described the hardships these people faced, and accepted as almost routine, in their daily lives. These excerpts were copied as the original authors wrote them so none of their flavor would be lost. There are also true-life stories about gold seekers, big game guides and the missionaries who lived and thrived throughout the 1940s, 1950s and 1960s. The last chapter of this book describes the enormous impact the Peace River dam, completed in 1968, had on the area and its people.

The men and women that lived and worked in this Rocky Mountain Trench area and particularly the rivermen themselves were a hardy lot. They were individualistic and resourceful in emergencies and they just loved to be living and working in the wilderness. These are their stories.

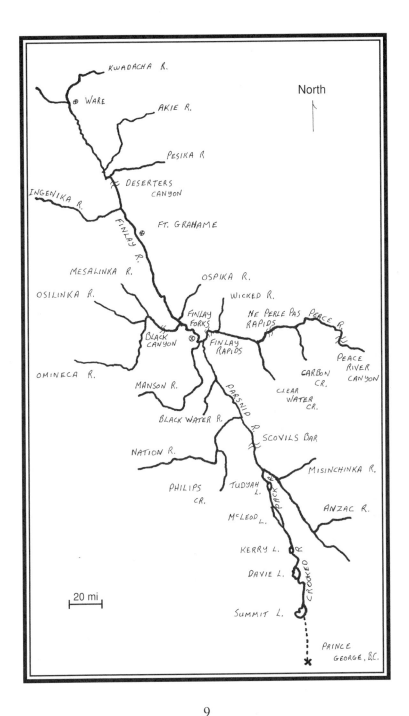

The River Rats

For twelve hours the men had been poling, pushing and dragging their heavy craft upstream against the current of the Finlay River. Ben Corke and Jimmy Nelson could line the long riverboat in some places by walking along the sandbars. With one man on a long rope that was tied to the boat's stern and the other on a shorter line tied to the bow, they would hold the boat on a slight angle into the current. The current held the boat in the deeper water and, with great effort, the men could make better progress walking than by poling. (Outboard engines had not yet come into common use in the early 1920s; price was a big factor. It was said that a dollar was so rare that when a man saw one it looked as big as a horse blanket.)

Tired and wet, the rivermen made camp that evening and could still look downriver a few miles and see the hill where they had camped the previous night. Slow progress—but that is how it was for the hard-working men who made their livelihood in the lonely country of northeast B.C. just after World War I.

Ben Corke established a trapline near Ruby Creek on the Finlay River and went on in later years to run the trading post at Ingenika and Fort Ware, almost 300 miles north of Prince George. It was illegal at that time to sell liquor to the Indians, but there was no shortage of bootleggers in those early years. Ben, however, did not sell any hootch at his posts and, in fact, restricted the sale of yeast cakes to one per family per week in an effort to keep down the making of moonshine.

Ben dealt with a lot of characters during his years as a trader and to be successful he had to give each person a margin of trust in the form of credit or "jaw bone" as it was called. The Pierre Indian clan used Ben's store for winter supplies and many would ask for credit until their winter fur catch was sold each spring. One particular couple never seemed to have any cash on them and always bought on credit. Charlie and Anne Pierre became known as Jaw Bone Charlie and Jaw Bone Annie.

One winter morning another member of the Pierre clan came into Corke's Post with some fur to sell. He produced a rare dark marten skin. Ben exclaimed, "This is the blackest marten I've ever seen." He told the Indian he could pay him ninety dollars for the exceptional pelt. (This was a princely sum for a marten in 1945, considering it is a good price for a marten skin today, 1997.) As Ben pulled out the cash box, he noticed his hands leaving black marks on it. Soot! The cat was now out of the bag. Ben admonished the fellow for trying to fool him and only paid him the usual five dollars for the fur. The trapper's only comment was, "Okay, I tried, no big deal." It was rumored that when the extending of credit was getting out of hand, Ben would tell the Indians to go and start a forest fire. The forest service would then hire the Natives to fight the fires and those pay checks would enable the Indians to pay off their outstanding debts.

Ben had lost the lower part of one leg during the First World War, but that injury never slowed him down. He had two wooden legs, one for working and the other was his "Sunday go to meeting" leg. He had a few spare wooden feet made up for his work leg as the swivel pin that held the foot on was always breaking off. He would be walking the river and get his foot stuck in the mud or between two rocks and the wooden foot, rubber boot and all, would come off and float away. Once Ben was setting up his camp beside some Indians. He did not know any of these Natives, so he decided to light his own campfire a few yards away from theirs. As his new neighbors looked on, Ben calmly rolled up his pant leg and whittled off a bit of kindling from his wooden leg to start the fire—he had their attention. Ben had another trick he would pull on the Indian children when they came into his store in Fort Ware. With his pant leg down and his boots on, his leg looked normal. Whenever he had an audience of kids around Ben would take an apple and begin to slice it in four to eat. He would then swing his arm in an exaggerated arc and stick the paring knife in his leg; the astonished children would run home to tell their parents the story of the tough trader.

Ben had delivered to his store the first battery-powered radio anyone ever saw. He sold this new marvel to Alex Pierre and the entire Pierre family and Ben all sat around that evening to listen spellbound to the radio for the first time. The station signed off at midnight and everyone went to sleep on the trading post floor. At 6:00 A.M. the radio came to life on its own and scared everyone half to death.

The famous bush pilot Sheldon Luck landed his float plane on the Finlay River one day and offered to give Ben his first ride in an aircraft. Ben accepted but as they took off he began to get mighty nervous. At this point Sheldon discovered his rear rudder was not responding and frantically tried to work the control. He turned to look back at his passenger and, lo and behold, Ben had a death grip on the control rod that ran overhead to the rear of the airplane.

Like most trappers that lived and worked in the Rocky Mountain Trench, Ben Corke owned working dogs. He had a big Mackenzie husky that could pack two medium beavers at a time, one on each side. He also owned a dog that was nearly the death of him. The dog had a bad habit of chasing bears until the bear would tire of running and turn on the dog, which, of course, would come running back to his master. He came running up to Ben one time with a grizzly in tow. Ben carried a big handgun and fired at the grizz. The animal turned and ran off. Ben surmised that he had only grazed the big animal. The following year the same dog came back again with a grizzly hot on his tail but this time Ben was armed with his .30/30 Winchester. He noticed the bear came with one front leg lifted up and this was slowing

the bear down enough that Ben had no trouble shooting the animal dead. Sure enough, it was the same bear; he had shot it through the first joint above the paw the previous year. "I'd had enough of that trouble-making dog," he told everyone, "and I shot him too!"

Corke was crusty, and on one trip through the Devil's Elbow on the Finlay he proved it. This was a very tricky bend and one wrong move here could put a riverboat and its occupants under a drift pile of logs. Ben and his stepson Ken Christopher were running up the Elbow using Ken's thirty-foot riverboat powered by a P-35 Johnson outboard. All of a sudden the head of the spark plug wire on one piston fell off and the other firing piston could not hold the boat in the strong current. Ben ran to the stern where Ken was operating the kicker and held the bare wire end on top of the spark plug with his thumb. The engine roared back to full power and Ken ran the boat up river the final 500 yards to safety. The whole while old Ben was absorbing continuous 10,000-volt jolts through his body from the powerful magneto of the outboard. Ben was sick for a full day afterward from the severe shocking his old bones had taken.

Trappers and prospectors of Scandinavian heritage came into the Rocky Mountain Trench area by ascending the Peace River from Hudson Hope. They had to portage over the Peace Canyon and work their way up rapids in the Ne Perle Pas and Finlay Rivers. Some found the country too hard and left after only one winter, the hardy ones stayed on trapping in winter and prospecting in summer. The odd one struck it rich. Gus Ola was one. He must have been an excellent riverman as he prospected up the Ingenika River, a tributary of the Finlay that is very fast in its upper reaches. The Ingenika comes equipped with more than its share of dangerous drift piles protruding out into the current. These obstacles can snare a boat and flip it in an instant. Gus struck it rich and sold out to a big mining corporation for $160,000—a huge sum in those days. He was to be paid this amount over a three-year period. He came to Prince George and stayed in the cheapest hotel in town, as was his habit. He began to distrust his friends, thinking they were after his money, and no doubt some were. He pulled out and moved to Vancouver where he was killed in a car accident six months after his strike. As Gus had no next of kin, the government got most of his money.

Some of these early rivermen settled down in the country. Frank Eklunt, a Finn, helped build the original community of Finlay Forks where the Parsnip and Finlay Rivers meet to form the Peace. Little Frank, as he was known, built his two-story house four miles up from the Forks. He was held in high esteem as an honest, hard-working man by all who knew him. The Ospika River drains the Rockies and flows into the Finlay River north of Finlay Forks. This river and the country north to Dead Man's Lake (Tobin Lake) were Frank Eklunt's trapping area. There is a canyon that had to be passed to reach the upper reaches of the Ospika. Frank kept a small riverboat tied above the canyon and in that way he did not have to run it with his larger riverboat. In the spring of the year high water made the rapids dangerous. Even in low water the canyon was tricky. When Frank got old, his declining health prevented him from trapping one winter. In order to keep on good terms with the provincial game branch, he asked another trapper to trap some beaver for him. This new trapper and his bowman had never run the Ospika Canyon and got a good scare here. It was navigable, but the steep chute on one section could be dangerous. The two rivermen were on their way back downriver with a heavy load aboard. As they approached the lip of the chute, the pilot could see that the nose of their long riverboat was going to knife into the big standing wave at the bottom of the mill race, possibly swamping the craft. He shouted for his bowman to get to the back of the boat to lighten the bow and the fellow scrambled back just in time. The riverboat managed to ride over the wave.

Frank was a bachelor, as were many of the early settlers in the north. Women were scarce. In the spring of the year Frank would head down south to Prince George for a little high life.

14

There were a few sporting women in Prince George in the 1930s who would entertain the men for a fee. Marie, Florence and Carmen each kept a house in town for lonely trappers and rivermen. Carmen's two-story house was down by itself where First Avenue was shadowed by a high bank. She had been having trouble with smart-aleck boys throwing stones from the bank behind her house onto its tin roof. A certain police officer named Frank Cook had been lectured by the madam to watch for these ruffians. It just so happened that Cook decided to park his car out front of Carmen's the very night that Frank Eklunt was visiting. Eklunt was no doubt engaged in a penetrating discussion with Carmen on the declining price of furs when the rocks hit the iron roof. Policeman Cook heard the commotion and decided to scare off the punks by firing a shot into the air. This was all too much on Frank Eklunt's nerves and he hurriedly left for the peace of the trapline. Meanwhile, Officer Cook had driven his car around to the road up behind Carmen's just in time to meet the boys. Collaring the oldest, Cook demanded to know what was going on. The excited boy exclaimed, "Nothing much—we were just throwing a few rocks down on the house and that damned pimp of hers came out and shot at us!"

Gus Dalhstrom was credited with being the best on the river with a pole, and poled his twenty-foot cottonwood dugout canoe for years before acquiring his first outboard motor. Gus had been a sailor as a young man, and it was on a square-rigged sailing vessel where Gus had an accident. He was working the ropes when his hand got caught up in the rope as it was going through a pulley; his hand was pulled through. Dalhstrom lost three fingers in the ordeal and forever after he was known as Seven-Fingered Gus.

Gus was a very successful trapper but a very poor money manager; in fact a lot of his profit was paid out to the provincial government via liquor tax. Gus had a habit of appearing broke even when he still had money. With his ragged attire he would bum a quarter off everyone he met in Prince George. He asked

"Seven-Finger" Gus Dahlstrom and Albert Huble Jr. in Dahlstrom's dugout river-boat on Summit Lake, B.C., in the 1920s.   *Photo: Al Huble*

one man for a quarter and when the victim gave him a one-dollar bill Gus gave the dumbfounded man seventy-five cents change! When Gus got old he did his own doctoring on himself. He was beginning to get chest pains and had a curious way of treating his heart. Once a day he would shake a little white crystal from a jar he kept in his pocket onto his hunting knife and lick it off! It was strychnine! Gus lived well into his seventies.

Delmar Miller came into Finlay Forks in 1911. Poling his dugout canoe, he eventually reached the Peace Canyon. He liked what he saw in this beautiful country and came back again with his partner, Bert Gregory, in about 1920 and set up a trapline near present-day Fort Ware. Joe (Shirley) Preston eventually teamed up with Del, and the two of them trapped the Finlay River country for many years. Del took a wife, Julie George, and raised a large family in the Fort Ware area.

Del was an excellent boat builder and was engaged by the Bedeaux Expedition to build whip-sawn lumber riverboats for exploration of the upper Rocky Mountain Trench. Del liked women; he was married several times. When he turned seventy-five years old, he married his third wife, also a senior citizen.

16

This new wife was quoted as saying, "Del learned how to run after he married me."

Edward Buchanan came into the country in 1925 from Montana with his wife and two children. Part of their trip from the U.S. was by immigrant train. The family was given a boxcar of their own that held all their possessions: horses, cows, chickens and themselves—all riding together. Ed, or "Buck" as he was nicknamed, had been in the Peace area as a worker on the threshing crews a few years earlier and liked it so much that he decided to move there permanently. Buck established a trapline on the Peace near Wicked River. He and his wife had two very young children along—Frank and Jean. It must have been a worry for them, so far from friends and relatives and days from any help in an emergency.

Buck ran his riverboat to bring supplies in for his little family and for the long winter on the trapline. He also got a freight-

Ed "Buck" Buchanan at Summit Lake, 1950s.   *Photo: Frank Buchanan*

ing job supplying the newly opened Ingenika Mine. Traveling from Summit Lake to the mine and back would take one week. The mine paid him seven cents a pound. He even hauled in a big air compressor on his forty-foot riverboat.

Buck used a dog team in winter to get around his trapline and to get his mail at Finlay Forks. Traveling the frozen Peace is not a cake walk. Thin ice occurs wherever the current is fast and at the entrance of side streams. Buck so proved his worth as a competent outdoorsman that he landed a rare salaried job as caretaker at Ingenika Mine when it closed. Besides the expensive mining equipment, he had to look after the horses that had been used to haul the ore cars. This meant not only feeding them but also keeping the numerous wolf packs at bay. There was a big natural hay meadow located a few miles from the mine site. Buck and his young son Frank would straddle a platform across two riverboats and load this up with hay to bring up to the horses at the mine.

In the 1950s, Buck moved his family to Summit Lake. The road construction crews were building the Hart Highway and Buck established a store to supply these crews and the local residents. His son Frank had taken over the trapline.

Fort Graham was established by the Hudson's Bay Company in 1890. The contract to supply this fur trading post was a coveted plum by all the rivermen. The company needed a dependable man for the job, as he would be in charge of the valuable trade goods and supplies. The chosen riverman would also be carrying raw furs worth thousands of dollars, so he had to be trustworthy. Lars Strom was given the contract in 1926, but he didn't last one trip before he was fired. Lars swamped his fully loaded riverboat at Long Riffle on the Crooked River when a backwash rolled over the stern after he ran the boat aground on a tight corner. Del Miller was a capable riverman and held the work contract for a time—as did a man named Gus Trap.

A big Dane by the name of George Jorgenson was finally given the Hudson's Bay Company contract. He ran it successfully for a decade until his untimely death in the fall of 1936.

One of the earliest photos of Jorgenson's river crew taken in 1927. Big Jorgenson is in the center (with suspenders) standing in the bow. Standing directly behind him is Louis Tereshuk. The man standing at the back of the photo (arms folded) is Jack Adams. Shorty Weber (wearing white shirt) is immediately to the right of Adams. The man sitting on the beach (at the right of the photo) is John "Slim" Cowart. Sitting near him (on the bow) is Jack Colberg. The others are unknown.

Photo: Don Adams

"Jorgy," as he was called, was a likable big man at six-foot-four and 240 pounds. He was easy to recognize with his big black hat and suspenders. Size was a good asset when it came to moving around forty-five-gallon gas barrels. Jorgy and his right-hand man Dick Corless built a boathouse on Summit Lake and, with an able carpenter named Jack Duncan, built a fleet of freight boats.

Jorgenson knew boats and was quick to improve on design if the change would make the craft more maneuverable or faster. A few of the residents around Summit Lake enjoyed racing their lake boats on weekends and Dick Corless decided to get in on the fun. He purchased a fancy, mahogany speedboat that had been built in England and with the biggest outboard made at that time, an eighteen-horsepower model, proceeded to beat the competition. Jorgy was seen inspecting this marvel of speed and soon built himself a cheap replica out of ordinary lumber. With this lighter craft, Jorgy handily beat his employee Dick at the next race.

Freighting by longboat was a tough business. Tons of freight had to be loaded and unloaded, not just at the various posts, but often to get through shallow water or fast rapids. One day Corless and Jorgenson were unloading 100-pound sacks of sugar at Fort

19

Graham and Jorgy had just placed a sack on shore. Turning to Dick, he said, "Well, that's the last for Fort Graham." These were his last words. Jorgenson fell over backwards stone dead. He had suffered a major heart attack. Dick now had to transport the body of his dead boss all the way back up river by himself to Summit Lake and Prince George.

Jorgenson had no next of kin, so Dick wired the Hudson's Bay Company for instructions concerning the fate of Jorgy's river contracts. The company turned the decision over to Government Agent Milburn in Prince George. The government agent was an important man in 1936. His duties included magistrate, judge of the juvenile court, official administrator, gold commissioner and official in charge of relief payments. Charlie Van Somer, who had been trucking the freight supplies from Prince George to Summit Lake for the rivermen, and Dick Corless were both interested in taking over the river-freighting business. At the height of the Depression interest in any kind of steady work was keen. However, with his past experience and excellent record, Dick won out over the competition and paid $1,200 for the riverboats, boathouse and the contract. This was a considerable sum in 1936.

Loading the freight boats at Summit Lake, 1935. The man in the center of the boats wearing suspenders is big Jorgy Jorgenson. The man standing at the right in bib overalls is Dick Corless. The building across the lake is the boat house where most of the riverboats were built. *Photo: Jim Van Somer*

Thus, marked the beginning of an era. Dick Corless went on to become perhaps the greatest riverman of them all. In a span of thirty years running the rivers, Dick only lost one ten-pound sack of sugar—a remarkable record.

Dick had been a hockey player in his youth and hired a number of men from his old team to bolster his summer river crews. Bull Nehring and Box Car Thompson were ex-players who worked for Dick. He also hired a lot of trappers as this was their off-season. This list included the Van Somer brothers Art, Jack and Jim. Bill Witter, Ludwig Smaaslett and Joe Berghammer were also trappers who doubled as river rats. Dick hired from some of the Indian community also. Two of his best bowmen were David Solonas and Harry Chingee. At one point, Dick Corless owned eleven riverboats.

Occasionally Dick would deliver more than $50,000 worth of fur from points north safely to Summit Lake. The fur was in bales and it was paramount that the dried pelts not get wet. He made sure it didn't. Because he was conscientious and dependable, he was in demand. Dick built up the business to the point where he had half a dozen forty-four-foot riverboats in service at one time. This meant be had to hire operators and bowmen for each boat. His payroll was considerable and he had a reputation for paying top wages on time. He was also in charge of delivering the Hudson's Bay Company operating money to be dropped off at various posts. This large sum would be for paying the wages of the Factors and their helpers. Each post also needed cash to buy the raw pelts brought in by the trappers. Dick would pick up the cash packet from the bank in Prince George and the manager was always worried it would be stolen or lost in transit. Prince George was a very safe town in the 1930s when the population was only 2,200 but the banker would tell Dick to go straight to Summit with the money. "Yessir," Dick would say as he and his bowman Walter Nehring would head for the bar for a cold beer before heading out.

Dick was described as a natural when it came to reading water; that ability to know where the deepwater channel was by observing the movement on the river surface. All the rivermen took pride in not breaking the propeller shear pins on the ten-day round trip from Summit Lake to Fort Ware, a distance of more than 700 miles return.

Dick had a good sense of humor. On one particular stretch of water as the Crooked River slows near Kerry Lake, there are many false channels. A sign had been erected with an arrow pointing to the main channel. A new man on the crew was coming upriver about a half hour behind Dick's boat, so Dick switched the sign. The false channel was a dead end about a mile up and ended in a mud flat. Sure enough, the green pilot took it and got stuck in the mud. Later on, back at Summit Lake, Corless asked with a straight face, "What took you so long?" Another time, he and Walter Nehring were once retained to take out three ladies for an overnight trip down the Crooked River. These women were not a very cheerful group and didn't hesitate to order the men around. When camp was made that night the women picked out the choicest spot for their tent and ordered the men to erect it for them on a smooth, grassy bench above the river. The rivermen did as they were told. In the morning the women were stiff and sore and one remarked how lumpy their beds were. Dick and Walter had spread fist-sized rocks under the tent the night before.

On another occasion, Corless was asked by a resident of Finlay Forks, Mrs. Johnson, for a ride out to McLeod Lake. She wanted to help with the poling and was seated about ten feet up from Dick who was operating the outboard. As this "bowman" swung the long pole from one side of the boat to the other, she hit Dick on the head. After the second bonk on the bean Dick said, "Give me that pole," and, taking his ax, chopped it in half. "There," he said and handed a useless five-foot pole back to the woman.

One summer Dick picked up a contract from the federal government to clear the rocks and generally improve Harrison Riffle, a bad shoal on the Crooked River. This shallow stretch of water was located about eleven miles downstream from Summit and was always a headache for the freighters. Dick labored on and off all summer, when not freighting, and rebuilt the wing dams of rock to funnel the water into one channel. He removed tons of rocks and debris by hand. For his efforts Dick was paid the grand sum of $150. His work helped ease passage here for a generation of trappers and guides who used the river, and the wing dams are still visible today.

The last trip north each year from Summit Lake to Fort Ware was made late in the fall just ahead of freeze up. On this last run the trappers employed by Corless would not be coming back out with the boats, but would be staying in the bush for the winter. This necessitated the hiring of extra men to man the boats for the return trip. The riverboats would be loaded to the hilt with empty gas barrels and a lot of frogging (pulling the boat) was required because of the low October water levels of the Crooked River.

Dick Corless hauled a mixed bag of equipment and supplies, including occasional passengers. His boats supplied the survey crews, government timber cruisers and pack train outfits. During the war years his boats supplied U.S. Army exploration parties looking for a rail route north and after the war the Hart Highway project kept Dick's boats busy.

The G. B. Williams Store in Prince George was where Dick purchased the groceries and supplies for the trading posts, and during the off season (winter) he worked for the owners as a delivery man around town. In the fall, Dick also did a little big game guiding, in fact he held a class A guide license for several years. (Class A licenses required a hunter had several years of successful guiding before being issued by the government.) He claimed he never made much money off of hunters, though. He told his brother Jack, "There's too many apple hunters from the Okanagan."

"Apple hunters?" Jack asked.

"Yeah, they only want to pay the guide in apples," Dick replied.

In 1958 Dick received a great honor. The province of B.C. was commemorating the 150th anniversary of Simon Fraser's trip through British Columbia. There were a number of big canoes done up in the old birch-bark style for a re-enactment of Fraser's trip down the Fraser River. The committee asked Dick to play the part of Simon Fraser himself. It was a fitting tribute to a great riverman of the present to the great riverman of the past.

Another one of the young rivermen of that era was Albert Huble. Al worked for Dick on occasion and also freighted for himself to supply his trapline on the Parsnip at Tony Creek, Pouce Coupe Creek and Six Mile Creek. Al's dad, Albert Huble Sr., had been active a generation earlier supplying Summit Lake over the portage trail from the Fraser River. He and his partner Seebeck used a type of Red River ox cart with six wheels to freight over this Arctic divide. In 1924 a road was built from Prince George to Summit Lake, so the Giscome Portage Trail, as it was called, was no longer needed.

Albert Jr. grew up with rivermen, trappers and guides so it was only natural that he followed in their footsteps. He began guiding in 1932 for a well-known outfitter named Curly Philips and went on to eventually acquire his own big game guiding out-fit on the lower Crooked River and Carp Lake area.

Al recalls the time he boated a big load of freight to Fort Graham. Included in this load was a considerable quantity of rum. It just so happened that the legendary horse packer Skook Davidson was at Fort Graham; in fact, he was there to transfer the supplies from Al's boat to the pack train for delivery to the mountains further north. Evidently the supplies, including the rum, were destined for a survey crew mapping the country. The rum never made it. A three-day party ensued with Skook living up to his reputation as a hard drinker. By the time the pack train left for the Kechika country all the cowboys were suffering from a glorious hangover.

Al, like most trappers, was an excellent riverman, and in 1947 he pulled off a feat few others would have tried. The contractor who was building the John Hart Highway from Prince George to Dawson Creek approached Al to see if it would be possible to freight a D-4 Caterpillar tractor. The road crews had reached Davie Lake and wanted to start a new gang working from McLeod Lake. Al built a platform across three of his riverboats and drove the big machine on top. It was the spring of the year and the Crooked River was in full flood. With very little difficulty, Al Huble delivered the tractor safely to McLeod Lake.

In 1925, a young boy of twelve years of age accompanied a riverman by the name of Ole Johnson into the Finlay River area. The boy's name was Jim Van Somer. Jim's father Charlie had been trucking supplies up to Summit Lake for the rivermen and Jim had been raised with tales of trappers, rivermen and the north in general. When the trappers came to Prince George in the spring of the year, the young boys would gather around and listen to their exciting stories. It was no wonder Jim decided at an early age that this was the life for him.

He started his trapping career with a trapper named Swigham on the Ospika River. The next year the first game warden in the area, Victor Williams, who had his main cabin across from Finlay Forks on Government Island, taught Jim to read animal sign and when to set his traps for the best results. Long hours on the babiche (snowshoes) hardened Jim up. He trapped and hunted beaver in the spring of the year and learned how to skillfully skin this animal, the toughest of all the fur bearers to pelt out without accidentally cutting the skin.

If a man trapped in the river country, he had to become adept at operating riverboats. Jim came to work for the river boss Jorgenson in 1936. It didn't take Jorgenson long to realize that Jim was competent at reading water and he was soon assigned to pilot his own riverboat. When Dick Corless took over the Hudson's Bay Company contract, Jim came to work for Corless and the two became the best of friends.

On one trip up river Jim had a passenger along named Jack Corless. Jack, Dick's younger brother, was only eighteen years old. Young Jack was full of enthusiasm. He was hoping to impress his older brother and land a job with the outfit. The boats left Summit Lake and started the difficult stretch down the Crooked River. Jack was in the bow of Jim's boat as they approached Long Riffle. Jack was instructed by Jim Van Somer to use his pole to shove the nose of the boat around when they got to the tight turn at the end of the riffle. As the bow reached the log bumper located there, Jack shoved his pole in a crack, where it got jammed. He instinctively ducked and left the pole behind. Jim looked up just as the stern passed under the pole and was almost thrown off the back of the boat. So much for the good impression.

By the time the boats reached the Parsnip River, Jack was in awe of Jim's expert handling of the big riverboat. At one point he asked Jim how he could tell the depth of the water so well when it was murky. He asked how deep it was at that moment and Jim replied, "Four feet." Jack looked at him as if to say "Yeah sure," and drove the pole he was carrying straight into the water; it was indeed four feet. Jim had been up and down the river for so many years he knew it like the back of his hand; as well, all the experienced river rats knew the telltale signs of shallow water. As the depth under the loaded boat shallows to about two feet, a noticeable lifting up of the entire boat occurs and a "bone" or wake appears near the bow. The shallow water also causes the outboard motor to slow down slightly as the propeller has to push harder to throw the water off the blades against the river bottom.

Jim, like Dick Corless, had an enviable safety record for all his years on the river. The other rivermen all liked Jim and there was a good general sense of humor among the crew. If a man did screw up, the rest of the crew usually got a lot of mileage out of it, like the time Jim's older brother Art decided to let his boat run itself. Art was piloting his riverboat down Cottonwood Riffle on Crooked River. He must have been looking down at his feet for nickels and dimes when a small sapling sticking out from shore knocked him off the back of the boat. On this particular trip there was no bowman aboard, so the craft just kept going merrily on downstream. Jim arrived in his boat to see Art standing in chest-deep water. "I lost my boat!" Art exclaimed. The runaway was soon corralled and the only casualty was Art Van Somer's dignity.

Jim went on to trap the Campbell River (now called the Anzac) with Jim Brandenhurst. Later Van Somer purchased a registered trapline on Chunaman Lake. This was a good fur-producing line and was well worth the $2,500 price tag. Jim Van Somer told me he had to run around Prince George that summer to tap nine different friends for a few hundred bucks each to buy the line. He also trapped with Ben Corke on Pine Creek and further north on Russel Creek with another good trapper named Bob Fry. When the Stolberg brothers got shot out of their trapping country on Bower Creek by a group of Natives, Elis Stolberg asked Jim if he wanted to take over. Jim wasn't intimidated and took over the trapline. "It was a waste of time," Jim claimed, "I never saw any renegade Indians, but I never caught even a squirrel either."

Jim did a little big game guiding in the fall and one year he took a hunter up the Omineca River through the notorious Black Canyon. They traveled by riverboat all the way, 150 miles upstream past Germanson Landing to Old Hogem on the upper Omineca.

Sitting in his trap cabin in the winter of 1942, Jim was listening to the war reports on his battery-powered radio. He didn't like the way things were going with the Japanese. At that time they were dropping a few bombs on the Aleutian Islands. He decided to enlist in the RCAF, so he strapped on his snowshoes and walked out 400 miles to Prince George. The Air Force said that they didn't need him at the moment, so he trekked back up north. Later on in the war his draft notice came up for the army. By that time he, Dick Corless, and Art Van Somer were busy freighting surveyors up river for the U.S. Army. The Canadian government had given the U.S. permission to build a transportation route to Alaska and the army was looking for a possible railway route up the Rocky Mountain Trench. The Canadian Army

decided the river pilots were an essential service and exempted Jim from service.

Like most trappers of that era, Jim had his share of close calls with thin ice and cold weather, but survived them all. He once took a young helper along with him late in the trapping season. Judge Robertson, from Prince George, had a son named Hal and this city-bred youth wanted to see what life was like on the trapline; so, he and Jim snowshoed into Jim's country on the Campbell (now Anzac) River. When they reached the main cabin Jim said, "I'll start a fire. You go down the bank to the river and fetch a pail of water, and be careful the river's deep here." He further warned Hal not to step out on a certain ice shelf that protruded out over a deep hole as this ice shelf was never stable. Jim lit the fire in the heater and then stepped outside to see what was taking the lad so long. There he was, right out on that ice shelf! Before Jim could say anything, the ice broke and in went Hal right up to his neck in ice water. The look on the boy's face was one of shock and disbelief. With help from Jim he scrambled out and no harm was done. Near tragedy was soon replaced with humor and they both had a good laugh back in the warm cabin.

Fate plays a big part in determining the outcome of a man's life. Jim's closest brush with death didn't occur on the trapline or the river, but in the air. He was walking out to Summit Lake in the winter of 1947 and as he reached McLeod Lake he noticed a ski-equipped airplane on the lake. After talking with pilot Pat Carey and engineer Ed Handwritty, Jim was invited to fly out to Prince George. This was a rare opportunity and would be Jim's first ride in an airplane. As the Junkers aircraft flew over Tea Pot

Mountain a snowstorm moved in on the plane and visibility was almost nil. At the same time the engine began to sputter—out of gas! The pilot had to make an emergency landing in a small opening in the forest that was nowhere long enough. The aircraft landed hard and just before it hit a wall of trees; one wing clipped against a tree and swung the Junkers right around 180 degrees. It then careened backward into the forest. This saved all aboard and everyone walked away from the crash.

In later years Jim got a contract to haul gas by riverboat to Cypress Anvil Mines near Finbow on the Finlay River. He would have to have a riverboat much larger than anything ever used before. In fact, it had to be able to carry fifty empty forty-five-gallon barrels at a time (less when the barrels were full). Jim had a custom-made steel boat constructed and had the distinction of operating the largest riverboat ever seen on the Finlay River— sixty feet long! Jim Van Somer's career as a riverman in the north spanned five decades, longer than anyone else's, a record that will not ever be equaled.

The postman in the river country had an exciting life compared to the man who delivered mail door-to-door in the city. The mail contract was held by Alan McKinnon in the 1920s. His job entailed traveling by horse from Hudson Hope to the Peace River upstream of the Peace Canyon. He then transferred the mail sacks to a riverboat and traveled up the Peace River over the Ne Perle Pas Rapids and the Finlay Rapids to Finlay Forks (seventy miles upstream). In winter the entire route was done on foot using snowshoes and a backpack. His trek in early winter necessitated walking the narrow ice shelf that protruded out from shore a few feet, as the big river did not freeze right across until later on. This danger was accepted as just part of the job. The mail was delivered in this fashion four times a year.

Quentin "King" Gething took over the mail run in the 1930s. King's father, Neil Gething, had developed a successful anthracite (a hard, hot-burning variety of coal) mine near Hudson Hope and King had grown up with the river freighters. King

Gething, like McKinnon before him, was a tireless walker and the little community of Finlay Forks could always count on King getting through with the mail. He used two riverboats and hired another good riverman named Bud Stuart to run the second boat. King's boatsmanship was so well known that he was asked by the contractors for the Alaska Highway to run freight boat on the Sekani Chief and Fort Nelson Rivers in 1941.

In 1937 King got an unusual request from the Anglican Church in Hudson Hope to boat some missionaries into Germanson Landing and on to Manson Creek. King had never been up through the Black Canyon of the Omineca River and was apprehensive about taking the three women and the parson, all greenhorns, along. He told the women the going could be rough and, sure enough, they soon found out when King ordered everyone out into the cold Peace River as they came to the Ne Perle Pas Rapids. King's outboard was only a seven-horsepower model, not enough to power the thirty-six-foot boat up against the strong rapids. With the four passengers frogging (pulling the bow rope) King operated the kicker and they made it through. The Finlay Rapids was a repeat performance, but this time the ladies first demanded King beach the boat so they could don their bathing suits and thus keep their clothes dry.

King told Parson Brown that he would have to be bowman and cautioned him to be ready. At one point a shallow spot was

reached and King wanted his new bowman to watch for the deep channel. The good parson was fast asleep in the bow. King was very soft spoken, hardly ever spoke above a whisper, and never got excited. He tried rocking the boat to get the man's attention but to no avail. Suddenly the outboard's prop hit the bottom and a sheer pin broke. The powerless boat immediately swung sideways and bounced off a rock. The parson came to life but it was a little too late. King managed to pole the long riverboat to shore for repairs and again reminded his bowman of his duties. King told the man to jump out into the shallow water and hold the boat steady if the sheer pin broke again. Parson Brown promised he would not get caught napping again. A short while later, as King rounded a bend, the outboard again touched bottom and the parson, thinking they were in trouble, jumped overboard—right into fifteen feet of water!

King came to the mouth of the Omineca and turned up the river. The lower Omineca was littered with drift piles and shallow false channels but the travelers had no problem here. The Black Canyon would be different. The water spews through this narrow gorge at tremendous speed with large boulders blocking the river's path. The parson was put on shore to pull on the bow line while the women stayed aboard to help, using the poles. Gething operated the outboard. As they were inching their way in this fashion, the bow rope broke sending the riverboat down-

stream sideways to the current and it was carried into a sweeper jutting out from shore. Luckily the boat did not capsize and King managed to pole it off without mishap as the ashen-faced women collected their wits.

The adventurers eventually got through the Black Canyon and after passing the mouth of the Stranger River (Mesilinka) and Swift River (Osilinka) they came to the Little Canyon of the Omineca. (I myself ran this canyon in 1988 with fifty horsepower available on my riverboat and can appreciate King's ability to do it with only seven horsepower.) The river in the Little Canyon runs down a narrow chute with a sheer cliff forcing the river to make a sharp bend. The six-foot standing waves have to be avoided by hugging the inside of the curve without hitting the protruding boulders located here.

Eventually the party reached their destination of Germanson Landing. As they approached the landing a large crowd of thirty people were standing on shore. The missionaries thought this was a wonderful welcoming committee for them but as they neared the dock a man explained that a float plane was due to land on the river at any minute, a fairly rare sight in 1937.

King Gething was a handy man to have around. He could fix anything with any old haywire material at hand. He once made a workable clothes-washing machine out of a forty-five-gallon drum and an old gas engine—a thing of beauty no doubt. He was a whiz at electronics and was often called to repair broken radios. When not running rivers, he and his partner Bud Stuart would go prospecting. It was typical of King to downplay any minor health problem in his later years, and in fact he developed diabetes but didn't know it. He and Bud were out looking for gold when King went into a coma. By the time Bud could get him out to a doctor in Mackenzie, he was about finished. Quentin "King of the River" Gething died at age sixty-four.

Art Van Somer was Jim's older brother and, like Jim, he worked for Dick Corless in the 1930s and 1940s. In 1947 the price of fur plummeted, and by 1949 the Hudson's Bay Company closed Fort Graham. At this point Art Van Somer took over most of the river freighting from Dick Corless. Using three riverboats, Art supplied the Hudson's Bay post at Fort Ware, and later the store run by Ben Corke.

When the old trapper Shorty Weber died, the job of cleaning out all Shorty's belongings from his main cabin fell to Art. Shorty, like a lot of other men who had lived too long alone, was suspicious of everyone and had become a recluse toward the end of his life. His petty feuds with other trappers were well known and this knowledge made Art wary as he approached the silent cabin. Rather than use the latch, Art kicked in the door and jumped back. With a loud clang, a big crosscut saw came crashing down like a guillotine to hit the floor.

Art was a quiet-spoken man who enjoyed a good joke. Art and Isaac Semore were running their loaded boat down Crooked River; Isaac was up front in the bow. When traveling shallow water the pilot always stands up for a better view of the river ahead to determine where the best route lies. As the stern passed under a low tree branch, Art failed to duck in time and was

Don Miller on the left with Art Van Somer at their trap cabin on the Finlay River, 1940s.   *Photo: Jim Van Somer*

knocked off the boat into the river. Isaac Semore looked back at Art standing soaking wet in the river and started to laugh out loud at his boss. A second later another low limb pitched him into the river too and it was Art's turn to laugh.

In the winter Art trapped and worked with some of the older trappers on their lines to learn the ropes. He eventually purchased a trapline on Paul Creek from a trapper named Art Blair. Blair had had enough after suffering several setbacks throughout his years of trapping. One of these setbacks occurred while bringing out his year's work of fur in the spring of the year. Rather than portage his fur and camping gear over the trail around Deserters Canyon, Blair decided to run the canyon at its worst—high water. He hit a big rock and flipped the riverboat. Blair stayed with his overturned boat, hanging onto the side, as it went round and round in the current. He could see his big bale of furs floating just ahead and hoped to save it. About five miles below the canyon he shouted at a cabin perched near the riverbank and, as luck would have it, another trapper, Bill Inesk, was home. Bill rescued Blair, but the bale of fur sunk.

When Art Van Somer took over Blair's line, Art's family came with him. He and his wife, Susie, raised three boys and four girls at the Paul Creek trap cabin and spent eighteen winters trapping the country here. Eldest son Bill followed in his dad's footsteps and became an expert riverman in his own right. Bill started running his own riverboat at sixteen years of age and to this day operates a tug boat for his barging business on Williston Lake.

The span of time (1910–68) that marks the heyday of the rivermen was short. The hard life these men faced often meant a short life expectancy, but it does not mean they are gone and forgotten, leaving no trace of their passing. Their exploits are retold through their descendent, keeping their memories alive. Also, some of the rivermen have had the honor of having streams and mountains in the Rocky Mountains named after them. They will not be forgotten.

Life on the River

What was life like for the riverboat operators on the Crooked River in the 1930s?

The Crooked River was the most difficult waterway to navigate of all the rivers on the route from Summit Lake to points north. For most people, riverboats bring to mind visions of large sternwheelers on the Mississippi. Nothing could be further from the reality of the Crooked River. This shallow river, and it could be more appropriately called a stream, required long narrow boats that incorporated special design features for shallow water travel. Young strong men were required to pull the craft through the shallows where outboards could not possibly be used.

Take an old bathtub and set it on a gravel road, load it half full of stones and attempt to drag it down the road. This will give some idea of what it is like to move a forty-four-foot boat with four tons of freight aboard down the Crooked River in low water—water that is maybe only four inches deep in some short stretches. River running was dawn to dusk hard labor. The men wore wool longjohns all summer long as they were constantly getting wet jumping in and out of the boat, and only wool would help to keep them warm.

The work began with the unloading of the freight trucks on the Hudson's Bay Company dock at Summit Lake. A lot of goods already came in canisters, like powdered milk, but loose food stuff was loaded into wooden grub boxes. Sacks of potatoes, flour and rice all had to be kept dry using canvas tarps. Heavy 450-pound barrels of gas were carefully placed aboard the boats. Care was needed for even weight distribution, and the barrel bungs (filler holes) were double checked to make sure no gas leaks occurred and contaminated the food.

The boats were on the water as soon as the ice was off the river in spring. This was the easiest time for freighting with lots of deep water available. As the season advanced, the water level

First Riffle on the Crooked River, 1930s. Four families of trappers heading north in fall to trap lines help one another out in low water. Martha Zlot is standing in bow with husband Tony holding the boats apart. Note wingdams of piled stones erected to direct flow in one channel. *Photo: Carl New*

dropped until it reached its lowest point in early fall. Whenever possible two or three boats would travel together so there would be extra hands available for pulling the boats over the shallow riffles of the Crooked in the fall.

The first shallow occurred near Tea Pot Mountain and was called First Riffle. In the spring these runs could be dangerously fast for the heavily loaded boats, so Dick Corless, the river boss, had on board each riverboat a forty-foot-long heavy chain. The chain was hooked on a post set on the boat's gunnel and was let out into the river as required. As the chain dragged along the rocky bottom of the river, it slowed the boat sufficiently so it could easily make the sharp bends at the end of these chutes. Second Riffle occurred only 200 yards after the first and Third Riffle only a half mile further. This third area and the Cottonwood Riffle that followed were particularly tough in the low water of late summer and here is where another of Dick Corless' inventions was used. He had a small punt (a flat-nosed rowboat) made that was used as a shuttle to carry small loads down the shallow water so the lightened riverboat could follow and reload at the end of each riffle. They called this little skiff the Bull Head after the man who ran it, Walter "Bull" Nehring. The Cottonwood Riffle had a particularly bad curve where the bowman had to pole the bow around a log bumper that had been

36

erected. His timing had to be just right, then the rest of the boat would skid off the bumper and continue downstream. If the bowman's timing was off, the riverboat might jam against the bank and possibly capsize.

Harrison Riffle was next on the agenda, followed by Scatter Riffle and Long Riffle. This latter riffle was ugly with lots of sharp bends and more than a mile of shallow water. In high water it was dangerous, and in low water it was hard, gut-busting work. If the big spruce trees on either side of the river had ears, they likely got singed a few times with the cursing that went on as the men tried to drag the heavy boats through the area in the early fall. This is where a riverman earned the $150 a month he was paid in 1938. Despite the low wages, rivermen considered the work an adventure, and there was never a shortage of potential employees.

Horseshoe Riffle was the last rapid to be negotiated. This riffle is where a cabin was located at a place called Lone Tree, which was about twenty-one miles below Summit Lake. When river conditions were really bad, the freight was taken down in loads as little as 1,500 pounds at a time and stored at Lone Tree until the last trip was made. (A forty-four-foot riverboat would typically carry in excess of 5,000 pounds of freight.) Rivermen had the consolation of knowing Davie Lake was just ahead and a welcome rest was in sight.

All day long the bowman was jumping in and out of the boat. The pilot had to lift his outboard up over the shallow spots and had to get out and help the bowman, as well. Sometimes the heavy gas barrels would be tossed overboard to lighten the load. The barrels would float downstream to be picked up after the shallows were crossed. With one man in the water up to his waist and the other on board, the 450-pound barrels were heaved aboard once again. In certain shallow spots the riverboat would be positioned across the river from shore to shore so it formed a kind of dam. As the water backed up behind the boat, it would rise and the resulting wash would carry it along for a ways; this would be repeated over and over until the shallow water was crossed.

Davie Lake was quite often the first camping stop below Summit Lake. This lake was called McKay Lake by the Hudson's Bay Company before 1900. Tents would be erected and a fire lit for cooking. It didn't take long for the men to hit the sack after that first day of travel. If the Crooked River's water level was higher, the first leg of the journey downstream wasn't too bad and the boats might carry on another ten miles to Red Rocky Lake before camping. This was more a widening of the Crooked River than an actual lake.

On the shore was the homestead of Louis and Marie Tereshuk. The coupled raised ranch mink and trapped as well. The Tereshuks had built an extra room at the back of their cabin just for overnight guests. There was enough room here for most of the river crews to spread out on the floor. This was a welcome relief for the tired men to get away from the worst of the mosquitoes. Louis and Marie never charged a penny for this hospitality and their children were always treated to candy by the rivermen.

On one memorable trip down river, the whole crew landed at the Tereshuks late in the day and Marie made a big supper for the men. She then prepared lunches for the next day as well. After she had washed the many dishes that evening, she excused herself and mentioned she was going into labor! About 2:00 A.M. a baby's cry was heard and little Rosie Tereshuk came into the world. In the morning the astonished rivermen found Marie preparing breakfast for the crew while Louis held the new baby in his arms!

As the riverboats progressed, the entering feeder streams increased the flow of the Crooked and travel became a little easier. Great care had to be taken when crossing the length of McLeod Lake. Sudden storms here would create five-foot waves, which were high enough to swamp the heavily laden riverboats. On occasion the wind would force the rivermen to seek shelter in the lee of an island on this big lake. Often it was a race to reach this shelter when the weather suddenly turned sour, and the crews might have to camp one or two days waiting for the wind to die down. McLeod Lake was the first location at which some of the freight would be off loaded. The Hudson's Bay Company Store and the McIntire Store located at the end of the lake near where the Pack River begins were both supplied by the riverboats.

McLeod Post is the oldest permanent white settlement in B.C. It was established in 1805 by the Northwest Company and taken over by the Hudson's Bay Company in 1821. This post was nicknamed Fort Misery by the early factors. There was very little game in the surrounding country, moose were nonexistent and deer and bear were scarce. This fort was on the Arctic drainage system, so there was no salmon run to rely on. Where the next square meal was going to come from was not always apparent, and starvation was not uncommon.

"Mac" McIntire was the Hudson's Bay Company factor during the twenties, but his conscience would not stand for the way the old HBC was treating the trappers, especially the Indians. He did not think the Bay was very fair in their trading and, as factor, he was caught in the middle between his employer's desire for profit and his desire to give people a fair shake. Consequently Mac opened up his own trading post opposite the mouth of the Pack River in direct competition with the Bay. He generally offered better prices for the fur brought in and would grub stake almost anyone. A grub stake included all the food provisions a trapper would need to see him through a winter's trapping season, and it was given out on credit. The trapper paid for those provisions when he sold his furs in the spring.

McIntire was very camera shy and few pictures of old Mac were ever taken. He always slept with his .45 Colt pistol under his pillow, his "hog leg" as he called it, but did not ever have to use it as far as anyone knows. When Mac's funeral service was held in the 1960s almost everyone from around McLeod Lake attended and many of the Native women were crying; they had lost a friend who treated them like family.

A character named George Holder helped run the Hudson's Bay Post at McLeod Lake. He was a great storyteller and led an

Mac McIntire at McLeod Lake, 1950s.   *Photo: Tom Ole*

interesting life. He claimed to have just missed action in the U.S. Civil War, but, in fact, he was born in 1865, the year the war ended—so in a sense he wasn't lying. He spent time as a youth in Old Mexico and had to "shoot his way out of a few scrapes." He never hesitated to show off his twin .45-caliber Colt revolvers. Holder never had any formal schooling; he couldn't read or write. Whenever anyone borrowed anything from George, he would draw on a piece of paper a picture of the borrower and the item he borrowed. This he would pin up on the wall as a reminder for himself. George was a salty old guy and never took any guff from the trappers and rivermen who came into the trading post. He was about eighty-five years old when a local was giving him trouble one day. The local was pushing the old timer around when George finally pulled out a big knife. "You siwash son of a...I'll cut you off at the pockets!" Later he told everyone, "That (guy) was a lucky man; if I had my guns..."

The Pack River begins at the outlet of McLeod Lake. The rivermen had to be careful on the Pack just downstream of Trout Lake (or Tudyah Lake as it is called today). This was where the cross-rapid occurred and if the channel was not exactly followed it meant more strenuous pulling on the lines. Where the Pack River enters the big Parsnip River, a delta existed (until the forming of Williston Lake) that could snare a freight boat on a mud bar. With even a little rain in the mountains the Parsnip became dirty, and these bars were hard to see if there was any breeze blowing across the water. Once on the bigger water of the lower Parsnip the bowman and pilot could relax a bit. However, eight miles below the mouth of the Pack was Scovel's Bar. Here the Parsnip fanned out across a wide gravel flat. In low water the rivermen might have had to physically dig an out channel with shovels to get through.

Brothers George and Bob New arrived at Scovel's Bar in a low-water year in the late 1930s. There were only four inches of water covering the bar. They set to work and dug out a channel more than 100 yards long. The job took all day and when the exhausted men finally got through it was late in the day. The two men pitched their tent for the night. All night long it rained and by morning the river had risen a foot. Such wasted work was part of the life.

All along the Parsnip River were various traplines, and supplies were sometimes dropped off at the trappers' cabins. Finlay Forks was the next major stop. A number of early settlers had located there after the first World War, including the McDougalls. Roy and Marge opened up a trading post there in 1925 and the store also served as the post office. The McDougalls were very hospitable folks and always made the travelers welcome. Mrs. McDougall was adept at first aid and carried some rudimentary medical supplies. The McDougall Post was as close to a hospital as most of the trappers ever got. Mrs. McDougall would call out on the wireless to the Indian Agent in Vanderhoof for medical instructions if it was needed. She bathed and weighed the Native babies, deloused the older children and dispensed cod liver oil to them. She instructed the Indian women on sewing and knitting.

One spring day a very sick trapper showed up at their door. Marge could tell he was toxic by his color. It seems the man had run out of lard to fry his food with so he substituted candle wax instead. This wax job really bunged up the unfortunate fellow. The cure prescribed by the McDougalls has been lost over time, but it must have been successful for the patient survived.

There was a certain Ingenika man named Alfred who was prone to irrational behavior. On several occasions he would strip off all his clothes and run around the village. He was finally brought down the Finlay River to Finlay Forks, accompanied by a couple of big Indian fellows armed with clubs. Apparently the mad man was caught molesting some children and frontier justice was prescribed. He had been beaten with the clubs and was now in need of medical treatment by Mrs. McDougall before being shipped out to Prince George.

Finlay Forks is so named because this is where the Parsnip flowing north meets the big Finlay River flowing southward. The two rivers come together and the Peace River is born. The distance from Summit Lake to Finlay Forks is approximately 175 miles, as the river flows. Most of the cabins, the trading post, a small mill and the radio house were located on the backwater off the Finlay River. The backwater was named Gibson Slough after the first man to open a trading post there.

Summit Lake, 1950s.

Photo: Jack Corless

One of the permanent residents of Finlay Forks was a trapper named Edward. As much as everyone liked Ed, they usually steered clear of his wife. This woman had a violent temper, especially when she had been imbibing the wobble water. On different binges she shot at Ed with her .22 rifle, tried to hit him with an ax and once bit him several times after she pinned him down on the floor. Ed was quoted as stating, "I don't mind when she shoots at me, I don't mind when she takes the ax to me, but when she chews me like a coyote, that's bad."

At one roustabout event, the notoriously bad-tempered Shorty Weber was nearly shot. He was innocently standing in the doorway of his cabin at Finlay Forks when Ed's wife went on the rampage shooting up the town. An errant shot hit the door jamb inches from Shorty's head.

Many traplines were downstream from Finlay Forks on the Peace River. Private riverboats would go down to the traplines, but commercial riverboats rarely descended the Peace, as most business was further north on the Finlay.

Fort Graham was north of Finlay Forks approximately sixty-five miles. This trading post was established by the Hudson's Bay Company in 1890 for exclusive trade with the Sekani Indians. The Sekanis would not travel to the Fort Connelly (Bear Lake) post for fear of attack by their traditional enemies, the Gitksan Indians, who resided in that country. There were about twelve cabins at Fort Graham and a Catholic church. The trappers from around the area went there with their furs, as well as trappers from the Ospika and the Ingenika River areas.

A lot of the freight would be unloaded at Fort Graham to carry the post through the winter. It was always a bit of an occasion when the boats would arrive; a crowd was usually on hand. The post factor would know almost to the hour when the boats would arrive as he could hear the outboards sometimes eight hours in advance. (In the 1930s the north country was very quiet. The airplane was rarely seen. There were no chainsaws, no elec-

Four riverboats unload supplies at Hudson's Bay Company Fort Graham, 1940s.
Photo: Jack Corless

tric motors, no generating plants and, in the Rocky Mountain Trench, no roads or automobiles. The early outboard engines were twin-cylinder with opposed pistons. They produced a chug-chug-chugging sound that in the cold morning air carried a considerable distance. The Trench runs north and south; and when the air was still, a man standing on the shore of the Finlay could hear the outboards when they were as much as thirty miles away!)

The bundles of fur pelts collected by Fort Graham would not be loaded into the riverboats until a few days later when the boats returned from points north. Twenty-five miles up the Finlay River from Fort Graham was Deserters Canyon. The freight had to be taken over the canyon's rapids in relays a little at a time. When bucking against a strong current the pilot would keep an eye on two points of land, such as one tree behind another, to gauge his progress. The engine would be running flat out and the water whipping by, but the actual forward gain might be nothing. The bowman was at the ready in case anything should go wrong; this was not the place to have the outboard stall. Once through the canyon, the going was fairly easy up to Fort Ware. But north of the Akie River, the Finlay braids out into many channels and a lot of potentially dangerous drift piles have to be negotiated.

As on the Parsnip River, the Finlay was home to numerous trappers and many of them got their groceries and other supplies from the freight boats. The boats regularly stopped at Bob Fry's cabin located twenty miles south of Fort Ware. Fry was seventy-two years old in 1934 but was still able to get around his trapline near Russel Creek. Often, he took young apprentice trappers under his roof to teach them the trade. Bob had a sharp wit and didn't hesitate to speak his mind. As Dick Corless unloaded Bob's canned meat one time, the old trapper complained that this was not his usual brand. The can's label read "Headlungs Meat." "They'll be canning arse holes next," said Bob. If you stopped in to see Bob Fry he would soon have the cribbage board out. Both Don Adams and Jim Van Somer spent a winter trapping with Fry and they began to suspect old Bob of cheating at his favorite game. Van Somer began to smell a rat when the old timer double-skunked him seventeen times in a row!

Sixty miles up from Deserters Canyon is Fort Ware. A trapper named Jack Weiser established himself at the mouth of the White Water River (now called the Kwadacha) before WWI, and later other fur traders came. White Water Post was renamed Ware in about approximately 1935, after Inspector Ware of the Hudson's Bay Company. Long tradition in the north pegged the word "Fort" in front of any HBC post, so Ware rapidly became Fort Ware. This was the end of the line for the riverboats, although the Finlay was navigable for another thirty miles up to the Fox River and farther to the foot of the continuous canyons that mark the upper part of the Finlay River.

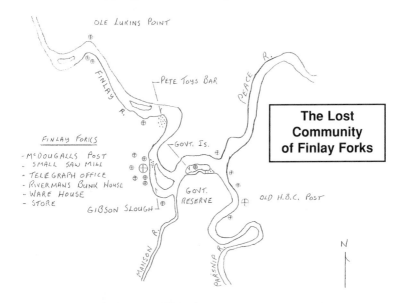

VOTER'S LIST—FORT GEORGE DISTRICT 1949
Finlay Forks Polling Division

Anderson, Samuel, trapper, gen. del., Fort Graham
Berghammer, Joe, trapper, gen. del.
Bird, Edward, trapper, gen. del.
Boyko, Marion, housewife, gen. del.
Boyko, William, trapper, gen. del.
Chalmers, Andrew, telegraph operator, gen. del.
Chalmers, Margaret Morrow, housewife, gen. del.
Charlie, Agnes, housewife, gen. del.
Charlie, Joe, trapper, gen. del.
Eklunt, Frank Victor, farmer, gen. del.
Johnson, Gertrude, trapper, gen. del.
Loveng, Gunnar, trapper, gen. del.
Miller, Sam, trapper, gen. del.
McDougall, Marge, housewife, gen. del.
McDougall, Roy, trapper, gen. del.
McPhee, William, trapper, gen. del.
Pierre, Judy, housewife, gen. del.
Pierre, Mary Sr., housewife, gen. del.
Pierre, Willie, trapper, gen. del.
Seymour, Juliette, trapper, gen. del.
Smaaslett, Ludwig, trapper, gen. del.
Smaaslett, Maggie, housewife, gen. del.
Strandberg, Edwin Claus, trapper, gen. del.
Teare, Morton, trapper, gen. del.
Toma, Isadore, trapper, gen. del.
Toma, Julia, housewife, gen. del.
Van Somer, Arthur, trapper, gen. del.
Van Somer, James, trapper, gen. del.
Van Somer, Susie, housewife, gen. del.
Vatcher, Margaret Richmond, housewife, gen. del.
Vatcher, Paul Ansteyl, telegraph agent, gen. del.
Warren, Milton Wilfred, trapper, gen. del.
Warren, Robert Omer, trapper, gen. del.
Weber, Frank, trapper, gen. del., Fort Graham

Courtesy of the Prince George Museum

I find it interesting to note that the sole farmer listed, Frank Eklunt, was a retired trapper. For younger readers, trapping was not then a politically incorrect profession. I also can't help but note that housewife, a nearly derogatory term nowadays, was an honored title then. Alas, the changes wrought by time are not necessarily good ones.

The Riverboat

The boat didn't look like much at first glance, lying there upside down and overgrown with grass, but it now belonged to me. I had purchased it for a very modest sum from a retired trapper named Bert Peterson. I would be using it for my trapline on the Salmon River. Bert had built this boat following the design of a Crooked River rat named Albert Huble.

We turned her over and I was happy to see the hull and interior were still in good shape after many years of outdoor storage. She was a short boat by river standards, only twenty-five feet long. But I could see the critical dimensions were correct—the narrow transom (a flat piece of wood that makes a square end at the stern of the boat), exaggerated out-swept sides, and above all the necessary fore and aft "rake" to the hull. A raked boat bottom has a slight bend upward as it nears each end of the boat.

We launched her in Hoodoo Lake, and I placed a small "kicker" (motor) on the transom. I started the outboard and took off down the lake. I was in my glory. It didn't matter that this was 1976 and not 1936. It didn't matter that I was on a small lake and not a big river. At that moment I was an old-time river rat on the Finlay River. So began my love for the old-fashioned riverboat.

Each major waterway in North America had its individual type of water craft. The mighty Mississippi had the keel boats of Davy Crockett and Mike Fink fame. These were poled along by manpower walking up the sides of the boat with poles set on the river bottom. The boats on the Mackenzie River were similar to those on the Finlay but had a much wider stern and usually had a wide scow type of bow because a pointed bow was not necessary on the wider Mackenzie. The boats used on the Crooked, Finlay and Peace Rivers were closer in appearance to the old York boats used near Hudson Bay by the early fur traders. The York boats were meant to be poled, and as such they were double-enders, i.e., like a canoe they could be operated in either direction. Some of the earliest rivermen, mostly trappers, used this type of boat on the Crooked River before the advent of outboard power. By cutting off one end and replacing it with a narrow transom, the first outboards could be used.

Gus Dahlstrom poled his twenty-five-foot riverboat throughout the early 1900s and into the early 1920s. He is generally credited with being the first of the rivermen to modify his boat in this manner, although the trader Jack Weisner built an inboard engine into a riverboat about the same time. Around about 1920, a group of men was standing on the riverbank of the Crooked one sunny afternoon when Gus came around the bend in his boat. Buck Buchanan was among the men on the bank and his words were quoted as follows, "Here comes Seven-Finger Gus and he's not poling. What's going on?!" Sure enough there was Gus standing up in the stern of his riverboat with a smile from ear to ear operating the first Johnson outboard motor made—a two-and-a-half-horsepower model.

Later more refinements were made to the riverboat by river freighters like George Jorgenson, Dick Corless, Slim Cowart and particularly a World War I veteran named Jack Duncan. In the 1920s a forty-foot boat could be built to the owner's specifications for a total price of a hundred dollars. A boat house at Summit Lake was built in the 1930s and many riverboats were constructed there by Jack Duncan for the freighters. These men designed a powered freight boat that could be used in small, shallow rivers as well as in the larger Finlay and Peace Rivers.

The sides of the boat tapered to a very small transom. This transom was just wide enough to mount the outboard motor. The narrow stern enabled the long riverboat to make the tight corners

Typical Riverboat

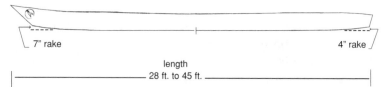

7" rake

4" rake

length
28 ft. to 45 ft.

on the Crooked and Pack Rivers. A wide transom would be continually banging into the bank as the long boats turned. Many times the boats would have to maneuver around log drift piles and, here again, a wide transom might get holed by a weather-hardened root or knot. The length of the craft was long in relation to the width. These boats had to be narrow to come down the Crooked River but still had to be long enough to haul considerable freight. A forty-five-foot boat might only be seven feet wide at midship.

I remember once when I was traveling down the Peace River near Taylor, B.C., a local man approached my thirty-six-foot long riverboat and remarked that it was the longest canoe he had seen. Indeed, these Finlay riverboats do look like a large canoe from a distance.

By far the most critical design element of the boat was the shape of its hull. The bottom of the boat was flat across but had a rise, or rake, not only as it neared the bow (as most boats have) but also as it neared the stern. This stern rake is a trait found only on the original Finlay design. I have seen this characteristic on the boats used on the Nation Lakes and on the Fraser River but its birthplace was in the boat houses on Summit Lake.

When a powered boat without the rear raking hull is traveling slowly through the water, it plows along with the stern drawing (that is, sinks into) considerable water, perhaps eighteen inches or more. It is only when driven at high speed that the vessel rises up or "comes to plane." The boats of the Crooked River had to be able to navigate in water as shallow as seven inches and the tight river bends precluded high speed travel, even if it was possible with the smaller outboards, which it was not. The stern rake allowed the riverboats to remain relatively level at slow speeds and thus draw very little water even with tons of weight aboard.

Finally, the wide angle of the out-swept sides helped the boats draw less water than today's pleasure craft. For every vertical foot, the sides would flare out seven and a half inches. As more and more weight was loaded aboard, the width of the boat increased its contact with the water to give more floatation.

49

The earliest river craft were constructed of sawn planks. These would shrink somewhat over the winter. Each year the bottom and sides had to be re-caulked with tar or pitch before the freight season could begin. Sometimes oakum (a loosely twisted fiber that is impregnated with tar) was pounded into the larger cracks. The transom block was usually made from a solid two-inch plank and sawed into the traditional V shape. In the 1940s, plywood was invented and this made construction much easier, and the boats were more water tight.

The Finlay is a silty river. When I was traveling it in 1988, I could hear the sand and silt rubbing along the sides and bottom. This silt and the general wear and tear on the wooden bottom from shallow water roughed up and slivered the bottoms of the boats to the extent they required sanding from time to time to de-whisker them. A noticeable speed increase was felt in a newly sanded and painted riverboat.

The boats were constructed in many different lengths reaching up to forty-five feet. But when plywood came into use, the boats were usually built in increments of four feet to get the best use of a four-by-eight-foot sheet of plywood. Tonnage or capacity varied with length.

Length of River Boat	Comfortable Working Load
45 feet	4 tons
36 feet	3 tons
28 feet	2 tons

Of course these boats could be loaded more heavily over short distances on calm water. They also had to be lightly loaded when going upstream into places such as Deserters Canyon. Jim Van Somer told me how he once had to make thirteen trips to get all the freight up through this canyon, loading and unloading the boat on either end.

The Corless' riverboats were painted marine gray color with the trim (inwales, outwales and rub rails) painted red. In addition, all Dick's boats had a flying goose symbol on the bow. The rivermen took much pride in their boats and the bow symbol was a distinctive signature of each boat's owner.

Ed Strandberg operating his forty-four-foot riverboat with a load of freight and passengers coming into Finlay Forks, 1957.

During the earliest years (prior to 1920), locomotion of all river craft was by muscle power alone. The first outboards, or kickers as they were called, were big, bulky machines of low horsepower. The two-and-a-half-horsepower Johnson and one-horsepower Elto were some of the first to be used. This doesn't seem like a lot of power today, but they moved the boats along nicely over lakes like Summit, McLeod and Tudya, and, with the men helping on the poles, they were a big help against the current in rivers. The Elto motor was unique in that the motor and propeller were fixed and only the rudder moved. Soon larger outboards came on the scene. There were the six-horsepower P-30, eight-horsepower P-35 and P-45, and the Johnson OK Series which were introduced in the 1920s—they provided six to seven horsepower. These motors were quite different from today's modern outboards. They ran at lower speeds and produced their power or torque by using large propellers. By the 1950s the motors ranged up to forty horsepower. All these were conventional propeller-driven motors as the jet had not yet been invented.

When running in shallow water, the riverboat's rear rake came into play again. As the boats were throttled down to pass over the shallows, where rocks could damage the prop, the nose of the boat would lower automatically, thus lifting the stern up and raising the vulnerable propeller higher. The rivermen also invented some ingenious means to further save wear and tear on the outboard's lower end. The jackass was a lever that when pushed down raised the kicker higher in the water while still keeping it in an operating position and running.

A few marine inboard motors were also used. These were quite a bit heavier than the outboards but offered better fuel economy and more power. Their disadvantage was that a fixed drive shaft and propeller remained under the hull. Even so, the rivermen used ingenuity and rigged up various adjustable U-joints in the shaft and rudders so they could be raised when operating in the shallow waters of the Crooked River.

By the 1980s, most of these long freight boats had been beached for many years. Wooden boats require a lot of maintenance to keep them from rotting. For years, several of the old riverboats could be seen exposed to the weather, pulled up on the bank of the Parsnip River, where the Hart Highway crosses. Many were turned into planters, high and dry in people's yards. Lately, however, I've noticed a renewed interest in the old-fashioned boats and with good reason. They are still the best design when large loads are to be moved. A new wrinkle has been added by some builders in that a few are using aluminum instead of plywood for the hull construction. I saw the first aluminum riverboats on the Nation Lakes at Chuchi Lake Lodge in 1983. The owner had built three thirty-footers and, except for being aluminum, they were the old Finlay River design. I retired my thirty-six-foot plywood river boat in 1989 and built an identical model out of aluminum for the 1990 season. My friend and fellow outfitter Scott Pichette just had a new aluminum thirty-footer built, true to the design, for use on the Bowron River located forty miles east of Prince George. The old riverboat lives on.

Trappers—The Early Years

No story of the rivermen would be complete without a discussion on the trappers of that era. Trapping is the occupation that opened up all of northern B.C., and the vast majority of the commerce carried out in the first part of this century was connected to the trapping industry. The existence of Forts McLeod, Graham and Ware were solely due to the abundance of wild furbearers. During the early part of this century when a man couldn't find a good-paying job to save his life, he could always go trapping to keep his family fed. A perusal over the voters list for Finlay Forks in 1949 reveals a total of thirty-four people registered. Of the twenty-three men, twenty listed their occupation as trapper, as did two of the eleven women.

This is how the job would have appeared in the want ads of a paper. WANTED: Strong young man to work in cold, harsh weather. Must be prepared to toil from dawn to dusk outdoors and in the evenings work indoors skinning and preparing pelts. Applicant will be expected to endure complete solitude for at least five months at a time. He must be in top physical shape for the continuous snowshoeing required and the heavy backpack he will be carrying. He must be able to subsist on short rations and, in fact, will be required to live off the land to a great extent. Above all, he must be adept at reading water and running river-boats. Pay will be meager.

If trapping sounds so tough, why do men choose this lifestyle even in today's modern world? I asked many of the trappers at our recent convention held in Prince George this past March (1997) that question and a common theme emerged. To a man, trappers enjoy the wild country, the wildlife found in it and the independence felt in making a living from it. I'm sure we could all make a much better living raising ranch mink, but that would pale in comparison to matching wits with a wild mink. Walk a high ridge in winter with a wilderness river valley spread out at your feet, the bright winter sun glinting off the snow—no further explanation is needed.

In the earliest years of this century, about 1917, two hard-boiled Irishmen by the name of Jock O'Rourke and Bill Krebs left Summit Lake in a handmade scow carrying food, traps, tin stove, rifles, ammunition, axes, crosscut saws, heavy winter clothing in duffle bags, camping equipment and everything else they would need to spend a year in the north. The scow itself would be taken apart once they reached the trapping grounds and used to make the doors and cupboards for the log cabin they would be building.

The two men drifted with the current down Crooked River sixty-five miles to McLeod Lake, twenty-five miles further down the Pack River brought them to the larger Parsnip River. Approximately another 120 miles down the Parsnip they arrived at a major junction where the Parsnip and the Finlay Rivers meet. Up to this point the men had a relatively easy time of it going with the current of the rivers, but now they would be fighting against the current of the big Finlay River, swollen with the spring runoff.

By sheer muscle power, they poled the heavy-laden scow up the river. At times, they would grab the willow bushes that grew alongside the riverbank and pull against these. They took advantage of back eddies whenever they could. Progress was measured in feet. They had to negotiate the mean Deserters Canyon by portaging all the supplies over the trail around the rapids and frogging the empty scow up the Canyon. For 180 miles they soldiered on against the current, averaging only four or five miles a day. Almost two months after leaving Summit Lake they arrived at their destination, the Fox River, covering a total of more than 400 miles. As they passed the mouth of the Fox, disaster struck. A crosscurrent from the river where it empties into the Finlay capsized their boat. All their gear was lost in the river. They managed to save themselves and the now empty scow.

The two desperate men reconnoitered on the beach over a fire to decide what to do. There was nothing else to do but retrace their steps back to Summit Lake. O'Rourke and Krebs did just that and amazingly resupplied themselves at Summit and headed north again. That epic feat has been remembered by generations of trappers whenever the going gets a little tough.

Edward Seebeck and Albert Huble Sr. were partners in the fur-buying business in the era before the first World War. Seebeck was a man who had tremendous endurance. Twice a winter he would make a trip by snowshoes from McLeod Lake to Fort Ware to buy fur, a distance of more than 300 miles. Walking behind his sleigh and team of dogs, he would guide the loaded craft down the ice of the Finlay and Parsnip Rivers. Often when the snow was too deep for his dogs, he would have to get in front to break trail through the drifts.

Every winter on a daily basis Ed faced the hardships of thin ice and numbing cold. Wolf packs would come into his camp at night and try to kill his sled dogs. In spring and summer he had to contend with swollen, fast rivers, cantankerous cow moose and short-tempered bears. Bears, both black and grizzly, would normally move off if a man came near—but not always.

It was early winter (November 28, 1921) when another riverman named Louis Tereshuk had an exciting encounter with a

bear. He was inspecting his marten traps on his trapline along Crooked River. "Trudging along with my pack and carrying a new .32 automatic, which I had bought that year," Louis said, "I felt I was prepared for anything that might come along. And it did. For there on the snow were the tracks of two bears—one set of tracks was mighty big compared with the other.

Louis and Marie Tereshuk with daughter Rose at their home on Red Rocky Lake about 1923.   *Photo: Viola Weatherly*

"I decided to follow the tracks left by the two bears, kind of wondering about the reason for them, and just what I might find. I laid my pack aside for faster traveling and started out, and the faster I followed the dual bear trail the more convinced I became that the two animals could not be far ahead of me.

"When I came to some scattered clumps of willows I was hardly as alert as I should have been. I got the surprise of my life when a grizzly, who must have been standing behind some willows looking at me, suddenly appeared on his hind legs, not fifty yards away and started shuffling toward me.

"I clapped the new rifle to my shoulder and let the bear have it between the forepaws. With the single shot I registered a bull's eye, for the bear staggered and crumpled to the ground. The bullet had split the bear's heart.

"After a cautious approach to the grizzly, making sure he was dead, I started to hunt for the smaller bear. Not far away I found a black bear which had been freshly killed, evidently by the grizzly, for the carcass was partially disemboweled."

Louis could now claim to have taken two bears with one shot. The animals provided his family with plenty of meat and fat and he sold the two hides for a total of seventy-five dollars.

The decade after the first World War saw a lot of men head north. Hollywood may have called it the Roaring Twenties, but times were tough for the northern communities. Young men were encouraged at an early age to leave home to look for work. Brothers Ivor and Ludwig Smaaslett were two such men.

Amazing as it sounds today, young Ivor was only thirteen years old when he walked into the Finlay River area with his dog as his only companion. Ivor must have been a confident, mature young man that summer of 1924. He returned to Prince George the next year full of stories of the wilderness and even had a fairly good fur catch to show off. His eighteen-year-old brother Ludwig was so impressed, he joined Ivor the next winter. Over the next four years their talent as trappers grew and with the price of raw fur holding good, both men prospered. Ludwig was an excellent traveler and opened up a remote trapline up in the Gataga River country. Ivor continued with the line he had established on the upper Pine Creek drainage. In spring, the brothers would travel down river together and both became adept rivermen.

On one occasion, Ludwig pulled the riverboat into shore, where a Native couple had a cabin. They walked up the bank of the Parsnip and the Native fellow invited the two young men in for coffee. When it was poured, he asked them if they preferred milk in their coffee. Ivor said he would indeed, but Ludwig, who had visited with this couple before, declined. Ivor couldn't figure this out as his brother always took his tea and coffee with milk when it was available. At this point the wife, who had been nursing her baby under a shawl, put the infant down. She picked up Ivor's cup and squirted a few drops of her breast milk into the cup. Ivor's chin nearly hit the floor.

When Ivor was eighteen years old, he became engaged. He returned to the Finlay area for the winter of 1928–29 trapping season and was to be married that summer. Alas, tragedy struck. While snowshoeing along the mountainous country of Pine Creek, an avalanche buried Ivor and his faithful dog. It was spring before anyone came to look for him and they found only the dog alive. Ivor Smaaslett was buried on his trapline in the country he loved.

Ludwig continued to trap in the winter and help the river freighters as bowman in the summer. He took on a partner named Fred Forestburg, and the two of them trapped some of the most remote areas of the Rocky Mountains. Fred and Ludwig were known as two of the toughest men in a land of tough men. They could carry tremendous loads into their mountainous country and, with very little store-bought food, would tough out the northern winters.

One winter Ludwig took Johnny Neilson into his trapline as a partner and John found out right away how hard it was to keep up with the long-legged Ludwig. At one point they stopped for lunch and John secretly loaded about twenty pounds of rocks into Ludwig's pack. "That should slow him down a little," John thought. As Ludwig shouldered his packframe he remarked, "This load is getting heavier all the time. I'll be glad when we get to the cabin." It hasn't been recorded what Ludwig had to say when he unloaded his pack.

Ludwig was known to get by on short rations and as Johnny Neilson was the cook

WENDY LIODE cci

he had to improvise at times. One afternoon while Ludwig was away on the line, John shot a great horned owl and boiled it up for supper. He told Ludwig it was chicken (a common term for grouse). After Ludwig had eaten his fill he remarked to John, "This bird has big bones for a grouse."

John replied, "If you think the bones are big you should have seen its eyes!"

Ludwig eventually married, and Maggie not only became his wife but also a good trapping partner. They

continued to trap and raised a family until the price of fur collapsed in 1947. That year Ludwig got a job in a small bush sawmill near Summit Lake and his employer soon realized how valuable a man Ludwig was. Ludwig had broken his lower leg but with it in a cast he took on the job of piling lumber off the green chain. The green chain was where the boards from the gang saw piled up in a heap. A lone man had to work fast to keep up with the sawyer and the machinery. The job was usually done by two men but Ludwig kept up all by himself, broken leg and all.

❖

Ed Buchanan and his wife Elsie trapped on the Wicked River drainage. The Wicked runs into the Peace River and Ed "Buck" Buchanan had trapline cabins along this big river as well. It has been said the north is hard on women and horses. Mrs. Buchanan was a strong, courageous young woman to keep her husband company on the trapline with two small children to care for. In 1930, she wrote a letter to her mother and in it she described the trip she and the children took with Buck from Wicked River to civilization at Summit Lake. This letter accurately describes what travel was like for the trappers of that day. At age thirty, she writes....

The wind whooped again from the east for two days more but on Friday the fourteenth we got away. The snow was whipped down hard to the Forks (Finlay Forks). We never put snowshoes on. The thermometer started up. That night it snowed a little again.

As I said, I was worried off and on about going out. All at once one day I thought how foolish I was. If I was to go, all right, if not that was all right too, and never worried since. Such a relief. One enjoys things a lot better. It's lots better to think that whatever comes, tomorrow is going to be lots of fun, whatever it is.

(The first leg of the journey was down the windy Peace to Finlay Forks where the young family stayed waiting for better ice conditions on the Parsnip River. By March fifteenth they were on their way again.)

We put all the dogs on the toboggan. The wind does not blow up and down the Parsnip. It is narrower and the mountains are far back leaving a wide valley and the wind blows over top. We found the going heavy. Broke a trail up about four miles. Decided we'd pack up and go to eight mile next morning anyway. So we did. Although Ed almost turned back after we'd all packed up. However we went. It got soft before we got there. The trail we broke was good. Found a one and a half mile open place. By the (river) edge was little snow or overflow so we got by there well. (Open water on the bigger rivers was a constant danger to dog teams). The last mile was heavy though. Ed and I broke trail and the dogs and youngsters just wallowed (the two children would be riding in the toboggan that was pulled by the dogs).

Ed went on and broke trail three and a half miles farther up that afternoon. It looked like rain farther upriver. Next day when we got up about six miles found a heavy crust on the snow where it had rained. We'd thought we would go a few miles and camp but found the going better than expected so we made twelve miles and arrived at Tony Zlot's place about two p.m. His young wife and fourteen month old son all greeted us. It was snowing next morning. They urged us to stay over a day and it did seem a bit foolish to start out when it was snowing with no trail so we stayed. Next morning we got off shortly after six a.m. It had crusted up some and was cloudy so we had good going. They offered us their dog which we accepted. A big black fellow, heavier than Mutt, three years old, never been used much. We lightened the sled and put him on it (tied him to it) alone. I never handled anything more like a bronco colt in my life. He was over the tugs and this way and that. Even now he ignores 'whoa' though I think he rather knows what it means. Poor fellow, his master had a very poor fitting collar for him and before I realized both his shoulders were rubbed bare. (They rigged a better collar later.) Our loads were pretty light as we had about used up our grub.

The day we left Tony's we made fourteen miles. Every day almost without excepting we found the going better. We arrived at an upper cabin of Tony's about twelve p.m. We stayed there.

Next day we made fourteen miles again. It was a bit harder, got soft early but we finished by 12 a.m. and stopped in an old cabin with a little gas can stove. We were all wet. It rained most of the night. The river was flooded about four inches of water lots of places. My rubbers beginning to give out but not high enough anyway, even with snowshoes. We made fourteen miles again, finished by eleven a.m. arrived at a large cabin (belonging to Al Huble). (That night the dogs got into a big fight with Huble's dog.) Finally after an hour of it I slipped into some clothes and went out. I found Ed had tied Molly and Mutt separately. Tied Molly by Mutt, tried to impress with a willow and returned (to bed). At four thirty a.m. we stirred. It had frozen some and was cloudy all day so it didn't soften much.

About ten miles up we talked to an Indian. He'd come down with a toboggan the day before for ten miles from his upper cabin. We went on his trail all the way without snowshoes which was quite a relief as we'd used them most of the way from the Forks up, almost to the finish of one pair.

We were only nine miles from the Pack River that night. We'd come over eighteen miles that day. Made Pack by noon. Camped in a poplar grove. Ed broke trail all afternoon. It didn't freeze much that night, rained a little, and then snowed a little. We moved only about a mile the next morning. We were all

Elsie Buchanan at Summit Lake in 1930s working her "plow horse."

Photo: Frank Buchanan

tired out. Ed said I groaned so he thought a rest would be advisable besides it hadn't frozen enough. It would be frightfully hard on the dogs to go anywhere. We left the river there and came overland seventeen miles to here. There was no place to camp after we left the river as we go through jack pine flats. So we only went about a mile, wallowed through willows into one back slough and then to another. There we used an old dugout to cross it as it was open. That took some time. A wet snow almost rain was falling. We finally arrived at the camp under two enormous spreading spruce. The wind turned north. The snow began to get colder. Soon it was freezing. We had to change our fly and fire then finally got settled but it was getting colder all day. We cut down a big dry spruce and kept a good fire. We retired early I assure you. We rolled out about five. I let the youngsters sleep with most of their clothes on so they did not have to get up till after breakfast. It was clear but cold nearly zero we were sure. Ed had broke the trail well for four miles; from there on we had a trail (a trapper named) Seebeck had made right through to here. We had a steep hill to climb. Ed and I put Molly and Mutt on the sled and took it up first then went back and took down the fly and got the toboggan ready. We told the youngsters to go up the trail as fast and far as they could. At the top of the hill we picked up the sled and with Ed at the handlebars of the sled and I on the toboggan we told Mutt to lead up and Mutt set the pace most of the way to here. The youngsters would run awhile and then climb on. Going through the bush one saves the dogs a lot by guiding the outfit by the handlebars. Also, there are numerous trees and holes to miss. We had a raising lunch and kept rambling. Arrived here about twelve forty-five. We never put the snowshoes on, the trail was frozen so well.

We stayed here today. It was quite a bit below zero this morning. There is a comfortable cabin here. The Hudson's Bay have cabins for trappers to use when they come. Only one here. In the summer it is occupied most of the time. We borrowed a tub and got cleaned up once more. I washed a few things but the urge to be on (the trail) is strong. We'll be moving early again tomorrow. I'm glad we planned to stop. Jean got too cold, I guess, yesterday and then over ate so she was sick in the night but feels pretty good tonight.

The wind seems to have changed so think the extreme cold is over again. It will help us through. The lakes which we must travel much of the way to the lake were flooded by the melted snow now they will be frozen well again. We have a fair trail all the way. Tomorrow night we must camp out again but the rest we can make cabins.

The children have stood the trip fine. We get up early but get through early too so most of the time we had several hours to rest in the afternoon and then turn in early - 6 p.m. for the youngsters. Seven to eight for us. I have always felt ready to go every day. I caught a few rides but not many. (When the going is easy, the musher can ride letting the dogs do the work). I walked and ran every step yesterday but felt fine today. I surprised myself. I got out every day for at least an hour before we started, some days longer.

There is lots of snow up this way but no ice in the rivers. That was Ed's worry. If we could make the Pack once all was well. Well we sneaked through somehow though in a number of places we had to take to the bank and travel over the gravel a ways and one place we used a long rope - taken for that purpose - and hauled the sleds by on thin ice where the bank was too steep. The old timers say they never saw a winter with less ice. Our dilemma was if we waited for the snow to melt there would be no ice left so we finally started anyway and think we did it the best we could.

I told Ed I could get along and not break my heart if he wished to go and leave us. Maybe it wouldn't but it would break mine he said, so I said no more. I didn't want him to feel he had to take us if it was too hard.

P.S. March thirty-first, four a.m. Arrived Summit Lake at nine thirty a.m. the twenty-ninth. Ed going in a hurry so no more till later. To me trail last out thirty miles (in) one day. All fine.

The trip from Finlay Forks to Summit Lake took sixteen days, a distance of 175 miles!

Before the registration of traplines in 1923, individual trappers worked anywhere they pleased and many disputes occurred. Sometimes problems arose between trappers, as they were very protective of their traditional area.

Harvey Scott set up his line in 1912 on a section of the Parsnip River. He came into the country from Colorado after his wife died. The beaver had been trapped and shot out over much of the north, including Scott's line. When registered traplines were established by the game department, no one but the registered owner could trap that particular area. This encouraged conservation and Scott had purchased mated pairs of beaver from the Provincial Game authorities ($10 each) to set free on his trapline. He guarded this fledgling population hoping to build them up to sufficient numbers to once again be able to trap them. Scott was considered eccentric by some and dangerous by others. Over a period of years, he had trouble with poachers and took matters into his own hands on occasion. A certain competitor named Weston disappeared one winter. Was it thin ice or did Scott know more about it than the police report indicated?

Scott was a hard man to get along with and had few, if any, friends. His father-in-law as well as Art Van Somer trapped with him one winter and they were always on edge. Both men pulled out earlier than planned when Scott showed them more than 500 rounds of ammunition kept under his bunk; they weren't sure just what Scott had in mind with all that ammo.

Travelers only stayed at Scott's place when absolutely necessary. Jack and Lucille Adams were once forced to ask Scott for hospitality when bad weather forced the couple and their two young children to spend the night. Lucille had to answer the call of nature during the middle of the night but discovered the cabin door had been locked with a padlock from the inside! She didn't dare wake cranky old Scott at that hour and had to use her tall riding boot as a lavatory.

Scott's sour disposition was a definite hindrance to him. He had to rig a lifting boom to pull his riverboat out in the fall as none of the other trappers would ever stop on their way by to help him with this annual chore. Scott was getting on in years, about sixty, when he broke his leg ten miles back off the Parsnip while checking his traps. He crawled back to his cabin and set his fractured leg by hooking his foot in the V of the loft stairs and throwing himself backwards. He almost passed out from pain but went on to splint the leg with kindling sticks wrapped with strips of cloth. It was six weeks before anyone stopped to look in on the old man. His wood pile was close by and he lived on jerky and beans. Scott was a survivor!

The north contained men who were far more dangerous than Harvey Scott. Too many years living alone may have tipped some over the borderline between eccentric and crazy. A "bunker" mentality could set in after a long winter—bush madness it was called.

One incident of madness saw Harry Holtmeyer shot to doll rags. He had been drilled nine times by a .303 rifle. The killer had waited in Harry's cabin, hiding in the loft, and let him have it at close range when he stepped through the door. Suspicion fell on Harry's trapping partner, a fellow Dutchman named Hans Christiensen, because Hans had vanished. Harry's body was found by a passing trapper named Shorty Weber. This event took place on the Peace River and Shorty related what he had found to the passing postman Allen McKinnon. McKinnon asked Shorty why he had not gone directly to Finlay Forks to report the incident. Shorty was evasive but finally replied that he panicked after discovering the body and just ran off.

One year after the murder, Hans Christiensen's body, or part of it, was found in the bush. He had been shot through the head, also by a .303 rifle. Hans was now eliminated as the prime suspect in Harry's murder as evidence showed he also had been shot several times—murdered. The police questioned all the acquaintances of the two men, including Shorty Weber, but could not crack the case and the killer was never found.

Another suspicious death occurred on the Finlay River below Deserters Canyon in the early 1920s. Trapper Bill Inesk was found shot, slumped on the floor of his cabin. Bill and Shorty Weber had been acquaintances; the word friend could not be used very often when describing most relationships with Weber. Who actually came across to the body first is unclear. Some of the local Natives, as well as Weber himself, were there for sure, and also a trader named Jack Weisner. The police put Bill Inesk's death down as suicide but others disagreed. The autopsy showed the bullet entered the stomach and traveled up into the vitals, a curious and painful way to commit suicide. Inesk's body had been found with a towel stuffed in the wound, indicating the victim had tried to save himself. Bill's cabin was located on the second of two benches overlooking the river. To this day, some of the rivermen believe Bill was shot as he walked across the first bench on his way to the river to draw water. A high bank, almost a cliff, overlooks the cabin from the opposite side of the river. A concealed sniper from atop this bank could have given Bill the lead poisoning. To lend credence to this theory was the fact Bill Inesk had placed blankets over the windows as if to foil a sniper from finishing him off. Like the Dutchmen murders, controversy surrounds the death of Inesk and unanswered questions remain to this day.

During World War II another senseless, brutal double murder took place on the Finlay River. Two men had immigrated to Canada from Germany or possibly Austria before the war and set up a trapline near Chunaman Lake. Eugene Messmer was an upholsterer by trade and Hans Pfieffer was a carpenter and excellent oil painter. They teamed up to build a beautiful cabin with handmade furniture and began trapping the surrounding country for a living. They enjoyed a good time and would invite the local Indians to visit their place and share their home-brewed whisky with them. WW II broke out and there was a fair amount of anti-German sentiment in the country. One fateful evening, one of their Indian "friends" named Coyote laid for the men as they snowshoed down the river. As the men returned home he gunned them both down.

A young traveler from the Omineca country named Don Gilliland was snowshoeing up the frozen Finlay River when he spied a big black dog circling a snow-covered bump on the ice. As Don came closer the dog barked and stood guard on the rise in the snow. Don calmly talked to the dog and got him settled down. As he advanced further, he discovered two snowshoes frozen into the river ice and the hair on the back of his neck began to crawl. He then recognized the bump for what it was, a corpse, and noticed dark stains on the ice. Don had known the two Germans from before and was trying to picture some kind of accident.

In Don's words, "...I became quite wary now. Sometimes in the northern bush a trapper or miner will go stark raving mad. Two trappers alone for months at a time could easily come down with cabin fever. The cabin came into view and there was no smoke. Still very cautious, I came to their water hole where they chopped through the ice. The ax they used was standing up in the snow alongside the water hole and frozen into the ice. This meant there was no one at the cabin, and that there had not been for at least ten days. It now appeared that the other partner must be sick, or possibly dead out on the trapline. I went on up to the cabin and entered the enclosed porch, but the door into the main part of the cabin was locked. I went around to the windows, but they were covered on the inside and I could not see anything. Surely something strange had gone on here."

At this point Don decided to report what he found down at Finlay Forks so the police could be wired. He again looked at the body and recognized it as Hans Pfeiffer and after giving some of his food to the starving dog, he set out for the Forks. He went to the government radio telegraph office and the operator informed Don that he had just received the same story from Fort Graham. Two trappers, named Jack Macguire and Jimmy Ware, had been on their way to Finlay Forks when they came across Gene Messmer's body on the ice. They turned back to where they had spent the previous night, where a third man, Ben Corke remained. The three then reported the killing back at Fort Graham.

Two British Columbia Police officers arrived by plane the next day and with Don and Marge McDougall from the post, they flew back up river. On circling the area they discovered another frozen body up river from the cabin. Don says, "We landed at the cabin with a hand sleigh and axes. But first the black dog had to be calmed. Marge knew him and had no trouble collaring him. He had been loyal to his master and stayed, keeping any wolves or other scavengers away. The dog was so thin that he must have been on guard for two weeks.

"After taking one body to the plane, we went for the other. At the cabin there was a snowshoe trail in the snow which was easy to follow. It led back of the willows, behind a big spruce tree, and down onto the river ice where the other body was lying...it was Gene Messmer.

"More pictures were taken, and on examination of the back of Gene's body, which was lying on its face, two bullet holes were found. He had been shot in the back! All this was noted as we lifted the body onto the hand-sleigh and took it down river to the plane."

The very next day the authorities arrested a Native fellow in the Finlay Forks store and charged him with the possession of stolen property. They had suspected him as the murderer and had found in his cabin more than twenty rifles and shotguns; one rifle was identified as Gene Messmer's. Upon further investigation the police charged the man with murder.

The B.C. Provincial Police, under Sergeant Clark and Constable McKenney, with the help of game warden Alf Janks pieced together the tragic events. The Indian had ambushed Messmer from behind, knocking the man down with two shots in the back, then coldly walking up to finish the victim off at point blank range. Pfeiffer was not as fortunate as Messmer. He had been shot in the right thigh with the bullet going right through the body. Pfeiffer had dragged himself for nearly a mile and died a slow, agonizing death.

Alex Prince, known as Coyote, was tried and found guilty. On November 28, 1945, the Sekani man was hung.

Other feuds were not as serious, but some carried on over several years. A certain trapper who was short of stature had it in for two others who had traplines near his. He sabotaged Gus Ola's outboard by sneaking in at night, unscrewing the spark plugs and putting a few small nuts into the pistons and then replacing the plugs when he was finished. Another poor trapper named Gus Trap couldn't figure out why his traps were not catching anything until he discovered a minute block of wood had been placed under the pan of each trap, preventing it from going off. On another occasion he returned to his home cabin to find all his belongings, traps, food, blankets, etc., thrown into the Finlay River. This was the last straw. Gus now decided to set a booby trap for his enemy. He rigged a crosscut saw over the door to be tripped by anyone who entered. It was supposed to fall on its victim. Reports are unclear whether the trap was ever successful.

The brothers Ellis and Hugo Stolberg held a good trapline in the Upper Finlay country near the Fishing Lakes and Bower Creek. At times Natives from Fort Connelly (near Bear Lake) would range into the Stolberg area and poach animals from them. Hugo was walking up to one of his sets one morning and surprised an Indian helping himself to the marten that was caught. The fellow panicked and, raising his rifle, fired at Hugo. The bullet broke Hugo's elbow. Ellis had to help his brother get back out to civilization for medical attention and was too intimidated by the incident to go back out on the trapline by himself.

Ben Corke once caught an Indian poaching on his trapline. As the Indian was bending over a trap, Ben decided to fire a shot just behind him to scare the fellow. Ben's aim was a little off and the bullet hit the trap the Indian was holding in his hand. The trap went flying and so did the Indian, never to be seen again. About a week after the incident, however, Ben spotted a fresh blaze on a pine tree. Written on the blaze was "Someday I fix you too Ben Corke."

Not all the trappers and traders treated the Sekani Indians fairly. Jack Blanchard trapped across from the mouth of the Akie River on the west side of the Finlay River. He would make his own moonshine and sometimes invite the Indians that were camped across the river at the mouth of the Akie over for a drink. On one particular binge he had a married couple drinking with him in the cabin. At midnight he kicked the man out but let his wife stay. The husband was drunk and half way across the river he took off his coat, rolled it up to make a pillow and lay down to sleep—it was thirty below zero! His friends and family found him in the morning; he was dead—frozen stiff. Blanchard was asked to leave the country and to enforce the eviction twenty Native men lined up along the river with rifles in hand. Blanchard pulled out.

The Indians from Fort Ware derived most of their income from the furs they caught and sold to the traders. One of the most colorful Natives was Chief Davie. He was a fine storyteller and possessed a good sense of humor. He would approach someone and state, "If I had a paper I would roll a smoke." When the vic-

71

tim handed over his papers the old chief would say, "I could roll a smoke if I had some tobacco."

A preponderance of the north's Natives are of mixed blood and many can trace their ancestry back to England, Scotland and Ireland. This is because the early Hudson's Bay Company factors and white trappers took Indian women for wives in the early years. One time when a big crowd was standing around a campfire the old patriarch Chief Davie announced that, "My daddy he was French Canadian halfbreed, and me, I'm same kind of bastard he are."

On one occasion a poacher had been hunting beaver on Chief Davie's line and the chief was not amused. The poacher had tossed the skinned-out beaver carcasses into the lake where they bloated and floated to the surface. The chief told his friends that he had discovered a whole bunch of "naked beaver" in the water.

The vast majority of trappers minded their own business and had no trouble from their neighbors; trapping itself held enough everyday dangers. A man can become disoriented in flat, heavily treed country on dull overcast winter days. The trapping cabins were usually built about a day's walk apart and if the next cabin was missed, the traveler was faced with bivouacking for the night under a spruce tree. The Muskovite Lakes country, a few miles west of the Finlay River, was where a trapper could be lost forever if he was not careful. A trapper named Gunthier was not careful. In late winter the searchers found his body. He was frozen stiff, still sitting by his long-cold campfire.

Some of the trappers had left skilled occupations for the lure of the wild life of the trapline. Jack Adams was a prospector as well as a trapper. He and his brother Bob had been very successful during the Klondike Gold Rush and the two men had over $300,000 to split between them when they pulled out of the Yukon. Jack settled in Finlay Forks while Bob went on to Czarist Russia. Bob managed to collect the proper documents and permits from the bureaucrats in that oppressed country. He and another partner spent a year prospecting in Siberia. As they were boarding their ship for home, the corrupt authorities detained them long enough to seize their sizable poke of gold.

Jack Adams was a highly skilled carpenter and log builder. He built not only cabins but lodges out of the native pine for other trappers and settlers. He built a beautiful home for a family near Gold Bar on the Peace River as well as several more near Summit Lake. He got summer work for the federal government to dynamite boulders out of the Finlay Rapids and even installed cables into certain rocks so the big boats could winch their way up these rapids. Jack's wife Lucille lived with him at Finlay Forks. Her first year there (1913) she never saw another white woman; in fact, she was the first white woman to live at Finlay Forks. Jack Adams was described as a "real gentleman" by all who knew him.

Jack and Lucille Adams had a son, Don, born in 1915. Don later became a riverman for the surveyors exploring the country. He spent a lot of time on the Omineca River and the gold fields near Silver Creek. He learned the trapping business from Bob Fry. As the two men sat in their cabin during the winter of 1933–34, young Don was practicing his quick draw with his old police-issue Webley .45 pistol. Old Bob Fry was beginning to get nervous with all this waving around of the pistol, "I hope you've got the iron sights filed off that gun," he told Don.

"Why?" said Don.

Bob replied, "In case somebody takes it away from you and pokes it up your backside." Don holstered his six shooter.

Don once related how the Natives were always leaving messages on blazed trees. This was the way trappers and families kept in touch before the age of radio—sort of the graffiti of the north. Some of these notices were comical. A jilted Romeo left a message on a tree near Ingenika. It read, "I go to Ware. No woman here."

The first official game warden to police the river country for game violations was an ex-trapper named Victor Williams. Vic resided permanently at Finlay Forks during the 1930s. He was well liked by most of the rivermen, probably because he would bend the rules a little. In fact no one could ever remember Vic pinching anyone while at Finlay Forks. Alf Janks succeeded Williams as game warden and was totally different. Alf enforced the law to the letter. He was once quoted as saying, "I would put my own mother in jail if she broke the law."

Once or twice a year game warden Alf Janks would check out the trappers. He was a good riverman himself and a tireless walker. He would snowshoe from Summit Lake to Fort Ware every winter to check for wildlife infractions. Until the 1920s, beaver trapping was not allowed at all, and when the season did open later on, trappers could only trap them from March to May of each year. Beaver were easy to catch in the fall before freeze up and some trappers couldn't resist the temptation to get an early start. Janks wasn't too popular with many of the trappers, including Bob Fry who had a cabin twenty miles below Deserters Canyon. Bob and his partner Jim Van Somer were in their cabin when a knock came to the door. It was Janks. Jim asked him how the trip up the ice had been and Janks' reply was that it was okay if you stayed in the middle of the river. To this Bob Fry replied, "Then why don't you stay in the middle of the river, nobody wants to see you anyway."

A certain forestry official was issued an identical car to the one Alf Janks drove. One evening just at dusk he was driving the car on the outskirts of Prince George when a bullet came crashing through the windshield. The forester could have been killed. He turned the car in and would not drive it again as he was sure the bullet was meant for Janks.

One winter Janks locked horns with trapper Art Blair. A man's home is his castle and Blair didn't want Janks snooping around his castle. When Janks went to climb up the ladder to inspect Blair's fur cache, old Blair spun him around and gave him a terrific punch in the face. This blow laid Janks out cold.

One of the most comical stories I ever heard about Alf Janks was related to me by Jack Corless. It seems Alf was motoring by riverboat down the Finlay River one day by himself when far ahead on the river bank he spied a Native woman bending over

some kind of animal. The woman had a calf moose down and was beginning to eviscerate it. When she recognized who was coming she sat on the carcass and spread her big skirt over the animal so it could not be seen. When Alf came up to her, he stated he wanted to examine what was under her dress. When she didn't respond, he reached with his hand to lift a corner up. The woman was holding a small hatchet in her hand, and taking offence to this invasion of her privacy, gave Alf a good smack on the elbow with the back of the ax, breaking the bone. Discretion being the better part of valor, Alf retreated and had to boat out to Summit Lake with a broken arm. He told everyone he had slipped on the river boulders but the woman had leaked the true story out and soon it was all over the country, much to Alf Janks' chagrin.

One crisp fall day Janks came across a hunter who had just shot and cleaned a mule deer near Summit Lake. The kill was about three-quarters of a mile from the road. Janks approached the man and asked him to produce his hunting license. The man asked, "Who are you?" to which Janks replied "I'm the game warden." The hunter was not convinced and asked Janks to show him some identification. Janks' replied that he did not have to show him anything. To that the hunter said then he didn't have to show anything either. The standoff didn't phase Janks. He said he was confiscating the deer, and charges would be forthcoming for hunting without a license. He then shouldered the animal and proceeded to pack it out to the road. The hunter quietly followed the puffing Janks out. When they reached the man's pickup truck, he produced his license and thanked Janks for packing out his deer.

Alf Janks had a policeman's eye for detail and his help was instrumental in getting the killer of the two Germans, Messmer and Pfeiffer. The police and Janks entered the cabin of one Joe Pierre where Janks recognized a homemade briefcase belonging to Messmer. Janks had made a point of knowing the weapons of most of the rivermen, and he recognized, in the cabin, the .300 Savage rifle belonging the Messmer.

Alf Janks was just doing his job and took this job seriously. His superior, Inspector Gill, described him as an excellent game warden. Janks was definitely not a desk jockey and would be out in all weather even when age was catching up with him. Jack Corless was traveling by car from Vanderhoof to Prince George late one night. There was a howling blizzard blowing so hard Jack was having difficulty seeing the road. Up ahead he could see a dim light. As he crept up the road, a man appeared with a flash-light in his hand; it was Janks. "What are you doing standing out here in this blizzard?" Jack asked. It turns out Janks had caught wind of a poaching ring shooting deer illegally near Cluculz Lake and was manning a roadblock in hope of apprehending the cul-prits on their way back to town. "I'll stand here all night if that's what it takes to get these guys," Janks explained.

The job of finding missing trappers often fell to the game wardens. When a trapper hadn't been heard from for a long time or failed to rendezvous in the spring, a search would be made. Inspector Walter Gill of the Game Branch was in charge of north-ern B.C. for more than thirty years. He is now a man of ninety-two years and recently related to me how his first job as a war-den was to find a missing trapper by the name of Basil Roarison.

Walter took two days to reach the cabin and found it locked. Quite often the early trappers would rig up a secret latch wire that would open the door. Inspector Gill walked around the back of the cabin and found a wire sticking out through the edge of the window jamb. He pulled it and the cabin door opened. He was filled with dread as he walked into the dark cabin because many trappers died from scurvy right on their bunks and he thought this is what he would find. The cabin was empty, however, and had been cleaned out of food and furs. Gill now began a search for the trapper's trail and found faint depressions in the melting spring snow that he reckoned were made by snowshoes. He followed these tracks to a small lake a few miles away. The tracks could still be made out as they crossed the snow-covered ice, but about half way across there was a perfectly clear patch of ice about ten feet wide. While the tracks went to this ice, none could be seen on the other side. Those were the days before RCMP diving teams and scuba gear. The trapper is likely still in that lake today.

On another occasion, Gill followed the tracks of a missing trapper/hunter until he came to where the man had tried to dig a bear out of its den. The trail then led to a small creek where there, frozen in the ice (with only his head and neck showing), was the missing man. The trapper's dog was still patiently waiting on the bank for his master to emerge. Walter had to chop the unfortunate fellow out and drag him to shore. Apparently the man's snowshoes had tangled in the willows at the bottom of the creek and the cold weakened the victim before he could extricate himself. Walter had a sheet of canvas with him, and wrapping the corpse in it, he dragged him off the mountain, the starving dog walking alongside the body.

Inspector Gill is a tall man—six feet five inches in his prime, but six feet two inches when I interviewed him. "A man washes so much dirt off his feet over the years it shortens you," he told me. Gill has a good sense of humor, which is always a good asset when dealing with the law. He told me that even though swans were and are fully protected on Crooked River, he was sure on a few occasions, while the guest of trappers, that he was fed swan stew.

His most humorous story was the time he had charged a hunter at Summit Lake with poaching a cow moose out of season; not only that but the accused was drunk at the time. Judges, unlike civil servants today, were not paid a very high wage in the 1940s. In fact, the judge hearing the case picked up a few bucks on the side by buying whisky during the week and selling it out of his house on Sundays when the liquor store was closed. He was bootlegging. The judge heard the charges against the poacher and bawled him out, not only for shooting the moose, but for the dangerous habit of hunting while intoxicated. "Where did you get that whisky?" the judge asked. "Why, I got it from you, Judge," the man replied.

The game warden's job could be dangerous. A regular police officer is dealing with unarmed citizens for the most part. The game warden however, is almost always up against armed individuals. Game Warden Feiry was sent to investigate the killing of a deer out of season. The alleged hunter, Frank Gott, was a World War I veteran who had been a sniper during that conflict. Feiry said to Gott, "I understand you killed a deer." Gott replied that he had indeed and that it was lying, "right over there." When Feiry walked over to check the animal, Gott gunned him down, shooting him fatally in the back.

A manhunt ensued involving the B.C. police and other game wardens. As the posse neared Gott they shouted for him to halt and fired warning shots ahead and behind the killer. One of the bullets ricocheted off a rock and struck Gott. He subsequently bled to death before they could get him out to civilization.

Inspector Gill recalled how the ticks were infesting the bush in 1940 and the poor moose were taking the brunt of the scourge.

In March some moose were too weak to get up out of their beds and others were too weak to move around much in the deep snow. They existed by eating the willows near by, right down to one-inch sticks. The ticks were the size of a man's thumb when bloated up with blood. The game wardens would douse any dead moose they found with coal oil and set the festering carcass ablaze. Gill saved a bottle of these pests to show to the brass back in Victoria. As he was driving down through the Fraser Canyon he felt a bite on the back of his ear. The bottle had somehow come open in the back seat of the car and the ticks were all over the place. Gill had to steam out his 1939 Plymouth when he got to Vancouver.

For most of the trappers, the season started with a trip to the Northern Hardware Store in Prince George to get outfitted. The Northern still to this day has all the gear that a man needs for an extended period in the bush. Alex Moffat used to outfit the trappers on credit, or "buckshee" as it's called, and would receive his money in the spring when the men sold their furs. Alex's son Harold told me they would keep a sharp lookout for the trappers in order to catch them before they whooped up their money in the beer parlors. Williams Store would also grub stake the trappers and even a new trapper could get credit here just on his word. The bush men were honest and the only time the store owners were not repaid was when a trapper died on the trapline.

It wasn't, however, always just for supplies that some of the rivermen and trappers lingered in Prince George. There were three or four brothels operating there in the 1930s. If the men tired of the beer parlors at the MacDonald, Prince George or Corning Hotels, they might wander over to Marie's or Florence's place. These were usually houses set apart from the rest of town, and the local police usually turned a blind eye to them as long as no one was robbed. Carmen's place was located by the Assman Slough near First Avenue, and for variety one could always go to Sarah's place. She was a black woman from southern U.S.A. and provided a few black girls along with the white ones.

❖

Many smaller feeder rivers enter the Parsnip and Finlay Rivers and up each of these watersheds is usually found an old abandoned trapper's cabin. A visitor today wonders who built these cabins and what kind of man would live in such isolated places. As raw fur held its price, even when times were tough in the 1930s, all these far-flung areas were trapped by hardy men. The Anzac River was one such area but it took a man in top physical shape to set up a trapline in the heavy snow belt area.

Jim Bradenhurst, Walter Scriver and Bert Thomas all set up traplines near this area in the early 1920s. Eight feet of snow is not uncommon in this area at the foot of the Rocky Mountains. Trails had to be continuously reopened, traps dug out and cabin roofs shoveled off to prevent them from collapsing. In the summer, big trees that had fallen from the weight of the snow plugged the trails and had to be chopped out each year. In 1936, George New took over from Bradenhurst. George's younger brother Carl bought the Scriver/Thomas lines. George and his other brother Bob had learned the ropes when working with Art Swigham on the Osilinka and with Ed Byrd on the Omineca in 1935.

The Anzac River is in bear country; the heavy precipitation grows tremendous berries and big bears to feed on them. George's wife Marjory got the surprise of her life one morning as she looked out the cabin window. There was a grizzly, standing on its hind legs on the porch! It was staring back at her through the glass with his nose to the pane. The bears would sometimes raid the cabins and steal the bait from the trap sets. When a bear starts he won't quit this thieving until he's hunted down and shot. The brothers had to protect their valuable food caches and each season

80

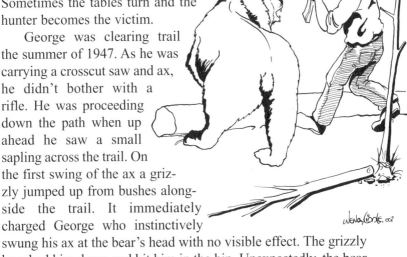

they had to kill a bear or two. Sometimes the tables turn and the hunter becomes the victim.

George was clearing trail the summer of 1947. As he was carrying a crosscut saw and ax, he didn't bother with a rifle. He was proceeding down the path when up ahead he saw a small sapling across the trail. On the first swing of the ax a grizzly jumped up from bushes alongside the trail. It immediately charged George who instinctively swung his ax at the bear's head with no visible effect. The grizzly knocked him down and bit him in the hip. Unexpectedly, the bear ran off, luckily for George. He limped back to his cabin and recovered completely. The following year George again came across a grizzly and shot it with his .30/30. As he skinned out the bear he noticed it had a scar down one side of its face—the same bear!

Many of the trappers who settled in northern B.C. were from Scandinavia. Trapping wild fur bearers has always been a means of livelihood in Norway, Sweden and Finland, so it is not surprising that the immigrants from these countries took up trapping when they came to Canada. A few Germans and Poles also pursued this occupation. A Pole named Tony Zlot arrived in Canada in 1912 and soon came to Finlay Forks. He prospected, trapped and freighted for the Hudson's Bay Company. He also ran a post for the same company. When asked during an interview what kind of motor he used on his boat in 1915, he replied, "Why I used the Hudson's Bay Pencil—a pole." There were no motors at that time. Tony stated that a good man on the pole could do twenty miles a day on the slow water of Crooked River.

Tony married in 1928 to Martha and she came to live with him on the trapline at Weston Creek, about fifteen miles up the

Parsnip from Finlay Forks. Martha and Tony had two children and were often isolated for eight months at a time. They would spend the summers in Prince George, but in September they would load up their riverboat with a year's supply of provisions and head for the north country, not to come out until spring breakup in May.

The winter of 1933 was long, cold and snowy. That spring the high runoff was nearly a disaster for the young family. Martha would check the river each day for signs of the ice moving. One morning it broke and the whole mass of ice started flowing. The Zlots would soon be heading out to civilization again. That afternoon, however, an ice jam formed a few miles downstream from their cabin, causing a temporary dam. By 4:00 P.M. the river was rising at an alarming rate and threatened to flood their cabin. Tony decided to load up his riverboat with food and sleeping bags as a precaution. The water continued to rise and Tony, Martha and her two small children had to get aboard the riverboat. They spent a cold night in the boat tied to a tree behind their cabin. By morning the river was another four feet higher and their cabin was in danger of floating away. The family poled their boat farther into the flooded forest to find dry land to camp on, but the heavy bush stopped them about a half mile from their cabin. For the next three days they lived on the riverboat! To cook their meals Tony tied up a floating stump to the side of the boat and built a campfire on it. Martha cooked the meals by leaning over the side of the boat and holding the frying pan over the floating fire.

On the third morning the ice jam broke, and the water receded so fast Tony could not get the boat poled back to the cabin before he ran out of water. The riverboat grounded out in the forest still two hundred yards from the river. Their cabin had floated away about a hundred feet to land on a stump and was now resting on a cockeyed angle. The woodshed had broken apart and all their firewood had washed away. The high water had almost reached their valuable fur cache eight feet up on poles.

The hardy women who accompanied their husbands into the north are often overlooked by historians. But in many cases, if it was not for the good women backing them up, the good men would not have made history. Mr. and Mrs. Johnson were among the earliest white couples to settle in the Finlay Forks area. Their trapping country was up the Manson River, but their home cabin was on Gibson Slough about a mile up from Finlay Forks. They enjoyed the quiet life of that beautiful area throughout the 1920s and 1930s until misfortune befell the aging Mr. Johnson. He could not pass water and in desperation tried to insert a catheter himself using the only thing available, a wire. Unfortunately, his rough attempt at self-doctoring caused internal bleeding, and even though he was brought out to the hospital in Prince George, he died a short time later. A lesser woman would have called it quits and moved to town but not Mrs. Johnson. Alone, she stayed on in Finlay Forks and continued to work the trapline. Even in old age she remained a strong woman, carrying a hundred-pound sack of potatoes from the riverboat up to her cabin and she only weighed a hundred pounds herself.

She was very frugal, as were many of her generation who had come through the Dirty Thirties. She raised a few strawberry plants in her small garden and would invite the young rivermen in for a feed when they stopped by. She was famous for making the berries stretch by beating them into a slurry and adding water. When she began to get too old to run the trapline she rented it out to a Swede named Ole Olson but she remained in the country for several years.

Childbirth, miles and days from professional help, was a stressful time for women in this isolated area. Crosses on small, unmarked graves near the cabins and settlements were testimony to the high mortality rate of newborns. Indian women who accompanied their men on the traplines often gave birth right where they happened to be when their time came. Bill Boyco was a trapper from the Parsnip River area. His wife Mary had all her children in the bush and all her newborns were very small at birth. Bill was quoted, after becoming a father once again, as saying, "This baby came too soon (like the others). Oh well, they all take the same size can of milk."

Popcorn Kate arrived at Finlay Forks from the Yukon. As a young woman she had been the madam of a red light establishment during the famous Klondike Gold Rush. In the early 1920s Kate arrived with her husband Charlie and settled near Finlay Forks. Not long after they arrived, Kate gave Charlie the heave-ho and moved in with a trapper and trader named Jack Weisner. This arrangement was without the benefit of clergy and was the scandal of the river country for years.

Kate got the nickname Popcorn Kate from two old trappers named Jim Rae and Bob Fry. It seems Kate was a big-bosomed woman, and whenever she bent over in her low-cut blouse she was on the verge of "popping" out. She was a middle-aged woman and was described as "hard bitten" by Bob Fry. Fry stopped in at Kate and Jack's camp one time and Popcorn offered to make tea for the men. It was the year of the rabbit boom and pellets were numerous on the snow. Kate didn't bother looking for clean snow; she just scooped the pot full.

As the snow water began to boil, the droppings came dancing to the surface. Kate just dumped the tea leaves in and poured out three mugs. When the disgusted Bob got his mug he looked over at Jack, but the nonplused Weisner stirred in some sugar and began to sip away. Bob dumped his cup in the snow when Popcorn wasn't looking.

Popcorn Kate helped Jack Weisner run his small trading post and the two of them were involved in a controversy when the trapper Bill Inesk died. It seems old Bill's fur catch disappeared sometime between his death and when the police arrived. All signs pointed to Kate and Jack. The couple was charged with theft and a court date was set. The prosecution met its match with Kate, however. She was brash and outspoken in her denial—you couldn't corner Popcorn Kate. The court found the couple innocent of all charges.

A very proper English couple immigrated from that old country and settled near the mouth of Carbon Creek where it enters the Peace River. Charlie and his wife Madge had a heavy accent and the locals at first made fun of them. Soon they won over the rivermen with their great hospitality. A passing riverman named Don Adams remembers stopping off at the Jones' home for a ten-minute break and leaving with a big hunk of fresh moose meat wrapped in wallpaper. Charlie, or "Carbon Creek Jones" as he was called, trapped but was a farmer at heart and he and his wife always had fresh produce on hand during the summer and raised a small herd of goats. In their inexperience with the north they built their cabin and garden too close to the river and during high spring runoff their place was nearly flooded out several

Carbon River Jones and his wife Maggie, 1927.

times. When they took their goats to market once a year it was, of course, by riverboat. It was a comical sight to see—twelve or fifteen goats perched on top of the duffel and running around the boat as it headed down the Peace River.

It may be difficult for people today, especially city dwellers, to comprehend why men and women would subject themselves to the dangers and deprivations of a trapper's life. In the 1920s, good-paying jobs were rare in the towns of the north and even rarer in the rural areas. Trapping was often the only means to make a living, albeit a modest one. Trapping's biggest asset was the independence it afforded an individual, and this occupation permitted a lover of the out of doors to live in the wilderness.

The Bowmen

By the mid-1920s the river-freighting business was brisk and Jorgenson, the river boss, needed able-bodied men to run his boats. John "Slim" Cowart was already an old hand at running rivers by this time, having arrived twenty years earlier. He was one of the first bowmen hired by Jorgenson.

Slim was born in Alabama in 1877. As a lad he worked on the cotton plantations doing that bane of the south—cotton picking. He wandered westward to spend his early manhood as a logger and teamster in the Portland area of Oregon. A tall man, especially for that day and age, at six foot five inches, Cowart was ideal for bull work. The young adventurer felt the lure of the north and rode by horseback from Oregon into the Cariboo country near Clinton, B.C., in 1900. His abilities as a horseman landed him the job of wagon scout for the freight business on the Cariboo wagon road. In 1906 he eventually arrived in Fort George. "Just a collection of Indian tepees beside the river," he once reminisced.

Wild fur prices were high and Slim traveled north into the Peace River country near Finlay Forks to seek his fortune trapping. He teamed up with George Wolsey who also came from south of the forty-ninth parallel. It was said that George got north of the border just one step ahead of the law. The two men set to work trapping the area northeast of Davie Lake along the Swamp River and as far east as the Parsnip River. This area had hardly been trapped, and in the winter of 1927–28 they caught 300 beavers off their traplines. Beaver pelts sold for $30 each in the 1920s—that was big money! Slim and George also became traders, buying fur pelts from the white and Indian trappers. The partners, at one point, amassed $50,000 worth of wild fur—a small fortune. Just before the traders could ship their fur out to market, the entire shipment was stolen.

The chase was on. Even though the police were notified, it would be up to Slim and George to catch the thieves if they expected to retrieve their pelts. Using dog teams, boats and horses, the culprits escaped, traveling across B.C., Alberta and the U.S. Slim tracked them as far as New York State before losing the trail; it was a remarkable chase. It was rumored that Wolsey's two brothers had followed him to Canada and were the thieves, but nothing was ever proven.

Slim also tried his hand at gold mining, but his success was only marginal. He worked as a bowman for Jorgenson until Jorgy had his fatal heart attack in 1936. During this time Slim formed a lasting friendship with Dick Corless and eventually asked Dick to be the best man at his wedding. In 1935, Slim was married to Hazel Bell at Woodpecker, thirty miles south of Prince George. Slim had reached the sensible age of fifty-eight by the time he married. Cowart was not a man to rush into things.

As the years caught up to Cowart, he spent his old age hacking out railway ties with a broadax, and also operated a second-hand store in Prince George. The city named Cowart Road after him. In 1956, at seventy-nine years of age, Slim Cowart ran his riverboat through the Pearly Gates.

The best bowman that ever worked for Dick Corless was Walter "Bull" Nehring. In my numerous interviews with the old river rats, his name continually came up. In his short life (he only lived to age forty-three) he made quite a name for himself. Walter was built like an ox. As a youth, he and his brother Robert played hockey for the Prince George hockey team. Walter and his brother were on the winning team of 1924. It was claimed that both were good enough to play in the pros. Bull was an ex-boxer, an excellent swimmer and a teamster for the horse loggers around Prince George during the winter months. He had big, thick hands and no one ever saw him wear gloves, even in the coldest winter months. He and his partner Shorty Hays started working as rivermen taking out geological survey parties on the Peace River in the 1920s. Moving the heavy boxes, barrels of gas and assorted gear in and out of the river boats was a snap for Walter. His strength came in handy in emergencies, too.

Bull Nehring on the left with Dick Corless, 1930s.   *Photo: Jim Van Somer*

Dick and Walter were on the Crooked River near Cottonwood Riffle during spring runoff. Dick was operating the kicker. As they were working their way around the sharp bend, the boat bumped and Dick fell out. The unmanned motor went to idle and the entire riverboat began to swing into a log jam. By now Dick was hanging on to the gunnel but could not pull himself out of the water. He was between the heavily loaded boat and the logs and was about to be crushed. Bull scrambled down the length of the riverboat, climbing over duffles as he went, and reached Dick as the boat was about to hit. With one arm he grabbed Dick by the back of his coat and heaved him aboard just in the nick of time.

All the riverboats required a bowman. His job was almost as important as the pilot's, especially on the smaller waters like the Crooked River. He sat near the bow until a difficult section of river appeared. Then he stood with his knees braced against the sides in the extreme front of the boat. He would watch for the deepest channel and would signal the pilot right or left. On tight corners he would push the nose around with his pole, no easy feat with a heavily loaded riverboat. He also kept an eye out for rocks or snags just under the surface that could take out the propeller.

In the early summer months the mosquitos were unbelievably thick along the rivers, especially in years of high spring runoff. It has been said that the mosquitos along the Parsnip River were so ferocious they would attack and eat a plow horse and then pitch the horseshoes to see who got to eat the harness. Out on the open water the bugs were tolerable, but on shore they were terrible, especially on an overcast day. The bowman often kept a few sticks of kindling and birch bark handy, so when the boat hit the beach he could immediately get a smudge fire going. During the first and second weeks of June, the mosquitos and black flies were particularly ferocious. When a stop was made to prepare lunch, the sandwiches were quickly assembled and then eaten on board back out on the river where the breeze kept the bugs at bay. The bowman was usually the designated cook for the ten-day return trips, and if the pilot didn't want to take over this chore, he learned to keep his mouth shut about the quality of the meals.

When the river current slows as the river widens, shoals or sandbars are hard to spot, particularly if it is windy and a chop is on the water. The old rivermen knew most of the bad spots, but the river channel never stays the same from year to year. The bowman had to locate shoals well in advance. I remember one time on the upper Omineca River in 1981, I was piloting my thirty-six-footer downstream with about 4,000 pounds of gear and passengers. The river forked and I accidentally took the wrong channel. No water! Before my bowman and I could turn her upstream the boat ground to a halt in about four inches of water. It took all hands out in the river to pull that boat around against the current, and off the sandbar. Two men alone could not have done it without unloading all the freight. The old freighters hauled much bigger loads than I had that day and couldn't afford this kind of mistake.

Some of the bowmen used a long paddle instead of a pole. Ludwig Smaaslet was the bowman for Art Van Somer and other rivermen during his years in the north. He sometimes used a neat trick to turn the long boats on a dime. When coming downstream on a river, if the pilot wanted to head to shore it was necessary to first do a U-turn. This enabled the captain to run against the current and come in slowly against the dock or shore. On a narrow river there would not be enough room to do the U-turn using only the kicker. While still motoring downstream, the bowman would place his paddle in the water in front of the bow and at an angle with the middle of the paddle shaft braced against the bow. A man had to hang on tight to the other end and brace himself for this maneuver as the boat turned sharply with all the force on the end of the paddle. Many a greenhorn bowman has been jerked overboard trying this stunt for the first time.

One of the funniest stories about the early river rats involved Bull Nehring; Jim Van Somer, Dick Corless and Art Van Somer were also along. Dick got a contract to take a group of five university students from Ontario's Upper Canada College on a sightseeing trip. He also had a genuine Count from Russia riding in another boat. Both riverboats ran as far as Deserters Canyon late one afternoon and the entire party stopped below the rapids. Count Ignatieff (a direct descendant of Czar Nicholas II) wanted to stretch his legs and look over the rapids from the cliffs above. Jim Van Somer tied his boat up to a forty-five-gallon gas barrel they had unloaded on the beach. As it was now late in the afternoon, Dick decided to set up camp for the night. They were sitting around the campfire swapping lies and no one noticed that Jim's boat had come undone. It drifted pilotless down the Finlay River. Finally one of the students noticed that the boat was missing. The camp went into instant action, and a search began using the remaining boat. The missing riverboat was not only loaded with freight and assorted gear, but also with the Count's metal cash box (reputedly carrying $2,000) and a bottle of rum. Four miles below the canyon near Red Ruby Creek, the searchers found the runaway boat up against a drift pile, sinking slowly. Only the front end was still above water. Bull climbed aboard,

On the Finlay River, approximately 1958. Left to right, Bob Van Somer, Bert Ware, Bill Van Somer, Art Van Somer, George Masatow and Mike Abou.

Photo: Bill Van Somer

grabbed the rum and leaped back into the other boat just a split second before the stricken craft sank. Dick stared incredulously at him and demanded to know why he hadn't grabbed the cash box instead. "What! And lose a perfectly good bottle of rum?" exclaimed Bull.

Corless hired a number of Sekani Natives as bowmen and they were ranked with the best. They were always coolheaded in emergencies and were strong on the pole. Jim Van Somer was the best riverman in Dick Corless' employ and always insisted that David Solonas, a Native from Fort Ware, be his bowman. David's brother Lectic Solonas also worked for Dick Corless. The other rivermen used to tease him about his name. They would tell him his mother called him Lectic because she got a shock when she saw him for the first time. Other excellent Native bowmen included the brothers George and Jimmy Masatow. George Masatow worked for Art Van Somer right into the 1960s, and was noted for always having a smile on his face.

1930s Crooked River—$50,000 worth of Hudson's Bay Company baled fur from Fort Graham. Left to right, Tony Zlot, Jim Van Somer, Bull Nehring, Don Miller, Enoch Towers. *Photo: Jack Corless*

Sam Miller, a Sekani Native from Fort Ware, was a good bowman for many years on riverboats, and a good canoeist as well. It was while practicing for a canoe race that Sam lost his life on Summit Lake. Sam and his partner, Glen Wilson, flipped their canoe on the lake and Sam, being a strong swimmer, made for shore. Glen stayed with the canoe. Sam made it to shore easily, but when he couldn't see Glen he dove back in to look for him. The swim back was too exhausting and Sam drowned—a courageous man. The wind eventually blew the overturned canoe and a tired, but alive, Glen to shore.

In my interviews with the few remaining rivermen, they all gave a great deal of credit to their bowmen for their successful careers. The pilot and bowman were a team; some pilots would refuse to move their riverboats without their regular bowman. Sadly, the bowman, just like the long riverboats he helped to operate, is now just a memory.

River Dangerous

The Black Canyon on the Omineca, Deserters Canyon on the Finlay River, the Finlay Rapids and Ne Perle Pas Rapids on the Peace were just some of the waters that separated the men from the boys.

Deserters Canyon got its name from the original explorers of the Upper Finlay. When Samuel Black ascended this waterway by birch bark canoe (the days of iron men and wooden ships) he made a camp at the foot of this canyon. It was June, 1824, and the Finlay was at full flood. The rapids were awesome with their haystacks (high-standing waves), whirlpools and boulders. All night Black and his men could hear the roar of the canyon. The thought of tackling this beast on the morrow was too much for two of his men. The camp awoke to find the two faint of hearts were gone; they had deserted. The canyon had its name.

The Sekani Indians that lived in the area always used the portage trail around the rapids. The rivermen got a chuckle when they reminisced about the time a group of Natives packed most of their gear over the portage, but decided to let the two canoes they were using just drift through the rapids on their own. One man was left above the rapids to set the boats adrift. After he determined the rest of the party was across the portage and ready to retrieve the two canoes at the other end, he pushed both canoes in. They came through all right—in pieces!

The run through Deserters Canyon was never boring. Art Van Somer was piloting his forty-five-footer up through the canyon, pushing against the strong spring runoff, and, as usual, the rapids demanded his full attention. Just as he passed the worst section he looked up and was appalled to see a moving mass of huge logs bearing down on him. A drift pile must have let loose somewhere upstream and now entered the canyon taking up the full width of the Finlay. That was probably the one and only time anyone ever

Rivermen coming down the Finlay Rapids located downstream of Finlay Forks on the Peace River.

backed down through Deserters Canyon successfully, a credit to Art's boating ability.

The Finlay Rapids were located just downstream from Finlay Forks on the Peace River. Jim Van Somer liked to give the "tourists" or newcomers a thrill here. To the uninitiated the rapids looked fearsome, but there was a good clear chute to take the boats through safely. Never show contempt for water, though. A Finnish prospector lost his life here during the War years. The game warden Janks and two other men were camped on shore at these rapids when the Finn decided to show off. He brought his small twenty-foot boat down through the worst of the standing waves instead of taking the safe route. The heavily loaded boat managed to ride up and over the first two rollers but drove right into the third. The boat and the hapless man were carried down into the depths and not a trace was ever found of either.

Even before the advent of powered riverboats, the river hazards were navigated successfully by muscle power alone. In 1920, a riverman named Bill Hedges pulled off a remarkable feat. He loaded his thirty-foot riverboat with 5,200 pounds of assorted freight and singlehandedly boated north from Summit Lake. Using only the "spruce driveshaft" (a pole) and oars, he worked this heavily loaded riverboat against the current of the Finlay River and arrived safely at Fort Graham. The trip took one month.

Black Canyon is located on the Omineca River, a major tributary of the Finlay, about ten miles upstream from the junction of these two rivers. This canyon was not considered navigable by most of the rivermen, but when water conditions were just right some made it through with their boat loaded light. Jim Van Somer ran through this canyon with a hunter he was guiding in the fall, and went up the Omineca another 150 miles to the Indian settlement of Old Hogem. King Gething also ran it a few years later with a boat full of missionaries and nearly lost the whole outfit.

Tom Batty knew the Black Canyon better than anyone else. Tom and his wife Winnie lived in a cabin near the canyon during the 1930s; Winnie's baby was born there. Tom was a prospector and during his years there he helped, on more than one occasion, any river travelers who found themselves in trouble in the rapids of the Black Canyon. However, some were beyond help.

Wes Gething and Bob Porter, prospectors from up Hudson Hope way, were trying their luck with the Black Canyon one summer afternoon. When poling or even under power, the boatman must never lose his bow. This term means to never allow your riverboat to veer too far off from facing the current flow. As soon as the bow begins to go off course, a correction must be made immediately or the entire boat will swing broadside to the current. This situation is not a problem if there is ample room to ride downstream and straighten the boat for another try, but in the Black Canyon there is no such room. Porter was at the bow with Gething in the stern when the treacherous current of the Omineca caught the bow and swung the riverboat downstream. The craft hit sideways against a rock and rolled over, spilling the two prospectors out. Bob hollered for Wes to, "grab hold of that floating bedroll, I'm gonna swim for shore!" Wes did as he was told and rode with the bedroll downstream to safety. Bob Porter was a wonderful athlete and strong swimmer, but his abilities were no match for the powerful Black Canyon—he never made it. Bob was buried on the bank of the Finlay River at Finlay Forks.

As bad as the rapids were, even more dangerous were the drift piles. In the spring of the year the high snow runoff would swell the northern rivers, sometimes over their banks. New channels were formed as the river cut through and around obstacles; in the process a lot of trees were washed off the banks into the river. These big spruce, pine and cottonwoods, with roots attached, would pile up on river bends and at the head of many small islands.

I was motoring up the Finlay in 1988 with my wife and children aboard and we came to a five-mile stretch where the river braided into many smaller channels. These channels wound their way around a myriad of small islands and each one had a drift pile at its head. I had to pick the deepest channel for the riverboat as well as watch out for sweepers sticking out into the current. In places the openings between islands were choked with logs with barely enough room to pass. If my outboard had given me any trouble as we passed in front of many of these jams I would not be here to write this book. A boat caught against them would be rolled under in a minute. Jim Van Somer was concerned enough that when he ran the Finlay he mounted a side bracket near the stern with a spare motor attached. As he neared a bad spot, he would start the spare motor and keep it idling. If his main motor quit, at least he could step ahead and rev up the spare.

A few years back a trapper and friend of mine lost his twelve-foot aluminum cartop boat in the Salmon River, just north of Prince George. He and his helper were trapping and shooting beaver from the boat when they were swept sideways into a small log jam. In seemingly slow motion the boat rolled under the logs and was bent in half by the current. Both men luckily were able to leap up on the jam just as the boat went under. They lost their traps, rifles, assorted camping gear, their boat and outboard. They also lost their pride but not their hide. When the waters receded later that summer the men went back to see what they could salvage. The boat looked like a piece of crumpled tin foil.

Ken Christopher trapped and guided for twenty years near Finlay Forks. His line went up the Omineca for a few miles. The Omineca is notorious for drift piles. He told me about one occasion when he was coming downriver in his thirty-two-foot riverboat. He had loaded up the boat with forty-five-gallon drums, stacked three high. Even though the barrels were empty, he had enough that the weight was considerable. Without a bowman he ran into trouble getting around a drift pile and sailed into it broadside. The current pinned him to the logs and the boat began to tip sideways, taking water over the side. Ken began throwing the barrels overboard as fast as he could and managed to lighten the boat enough to save it. He said, "You never saw a man work so fast in your life!"

A tragedy occurred in the late 1940s on the Anzac River. This tributary of the upper Parsnip River was being trapped by George New. The Anzac was swollen with the spring runoff. George, his wife Marjory and their two children were coming down in George's thirty-foot riverboat when he encountered a treacherous spot on the river. The dirty, brown Anzac was rushing headlong into a logjam that partially blocked the river. George was an experienced riverman and had negotiated around this obstacle on several previous occasions. The procedure was to approach the jam as slow as possible and, at a crucial point, gun the outboard motor to swing the boat hard around and across the face of the jam. The youngsters aboard were both less than six years of age and none of the party was equipped with life jackets (which were uncommon in the 1940s). Just as the riverboat came to the pivotal spot where George would power it past the drift pile, an underwater root hit the propeller breaking the shear pin.

George revved up the motor to no avail, and the riverboat careened into the logs sideways. Somehow the downstream side of the riverboat rode up onto the logs and the upstream side caught the full force of the rushing river. The riverboat capsized throwing all aboard into the fast water. Marjory was the first to rise to the surface and was mortified when she couldn't see the others. George suddenly popped up and got a grip on a log. The unfortunate children, however, were swept under the log jam. Carl New, George's brother, arrived on the scene hours after the tragedy and was able to free the riverboat, but no trace of the two children was ever found.

The Devil's Elbow was located below Red Ruby Creek on the Finlay. Here the river was blocked on both sides by drift piles that forced the river through a narrow passageway. It was critical, especially when navigating downstream, to correctly line up the riverboat for this gap. Strong eddies and whirlpools guarded the bend. Before the days of power many a boat was lost there. The river makes a hard turn (more than ninety degrees) and one wrong move could sweep a boat into the logs or the whirlpool.

A trapper named Gus Trap made the mistake of drifting down the river at night in a small rowboat. As he entered the Devil's Elbow, the big whirlpool spun his boat and Gus either jumped or fell out. The rowboat was found on a sandbar a short way downstream. Gus was never found.

The Ne Perle Pas Rapids, located about forty miles downstream from Finlay forks, were tricky, especially in the days before outboard motors. Around about 1918 two trappers decided to form a partnership for the winter's trapping season. Henry Stege and Jack Wiesner upset their boat in the Ne Perle Pas Rapids. They had been tracking their heavily loaded vessel

through the rapids when the bow line broke. The boat swung sideways to the current and swamped, losing all their gear. The men got to arguing over whose fault it was and the partnership came to an abrupt end.

A good riverman named Bob Beattie cut his eye teeth on these rapids while learning to handle a riverboat for the first time. He was just a boy in 1942 when he went through the rapids with two older men. The old-timers figured Bob was old enough to run the river and they let him take control of the outboard. As Bob piloted the long boat into the turbulence the old pros, sitting in the bow, pointed out which way to go, but at a critical spot they both pointed in opposite directions. Confused, Bob decided to split the difference and went down the middle—big mistake! A huge wave came crashing over the bow and swamped the river-boat; she slowly began to sink into the Peace River. By poling they somehow managed to guide the floundering craft to shore. Bob took a lot of passengers through the Ne Perle Pas Rapids during his years as a river outfitter and claimed he never lost a "pilgrim."

Ole Johnson lived and trapped the Wicked River area in the early 1920s (later selling his line to Buck Buchanan). He used an unruly, big, thirty-foot scow for a riverboat that was not very maneuverable in fast water, especially with the underpowered outboards of the day. He was attempting to run down the Finlay Rapids in fairly high water one afternoon and had as bowman a small boy of just twelve years of age. The boy was standing right up front in the bow when the scow side slipped into the mael-strom of the big standing waves. The boat rode the first wave but cut the second in half. The youth was washed off his feet and almost out of the boat; he wound up in the stern with Ole who desperately guided the barely floating boat to shore. The river doesn't win them all.

The Misinchinka is a fast little river that flows into the Parsnip just above where the Hart Highway bridge crosses the Parsnip today, about 100 miles north of Prince George. It was the trapping country of Howard Powell in the early part of this cen-tury. Powell had been out of the trapping game for more than fif-

Harry Copperwaite at his modest trapping cabin, Pouce Coupe Creek, 1938.

teen years when, at age fifty and out of nostalgia, he decided to revisit his old trapline. He hired two young men to take him from Summit Lake to the Misinchinka using their small riverboat. The boys were about eighteen years of age, but they were already experienced rivermen by this time (approximately 1931). Their names were Harry Copperwaite and none other than Jim Van Somer. Also aboard were Powell's wife and her small dog named Peggy.

About fifteen miles up the Misinchinka, a dead tree projecting out from shore hooked their three-horsepower outboard motor and flipped it off the transom into the river. The party now faced the prospect of having to drift back down the river with its many hairpin turns. With Harry in the stern and Jim at the bow, the men poled the boat down river. They came to a section where a big drift pile blocked off most of the river. With no power available, the riverboat could not be guided past the logs. The boat came up to the logs broadside and almost immediately rolled over. Harry and Powell leaped onto the drift pile, but the woman was swept under the logs. Jim was in the water, too, but was able to hold onto a small rope that had been tied to the side of the boat. The bow rope itself was wrapped around Jim's legs and he was having a hard time extricating himself. Harry Copperwaite looked with horror as Mrs. Powell was taken under. There was a small hole about fifteen feet downstream from the face of the jam where open water boiled to the surface and, all of a sudden, a sputtering woman bobbed up. Harry scrambled like a cat across the logs, grabbed her by the hair and yanked her to safety.

The party was now in a fine fix. The boat was pinned upside down, partially under the log jam, all their food and sleeping bags were lost and Mrs. Powell was crying hysterically. All she could say was "poor Peggy, poor Peggy." The men tried to calm her down, but without much success. At this point Jim noticed the riverboat give a lurch and right itself. Out popped the dog, wet but alive. Using poles as pry bars, Harry and Jim were able to free the boat and soon had it bailed out. A few miles of drifting down river and they found an abandoned cabin with a little food in it. They quickly had a fire going and the near disaster was behind them. All made it down river safely, including the dog.

In our modern world we rarely, if ever, have to face danger and certainly not on a daily basis. It has been said that a good scare shortens a man's life by a few minutes. When approaching a dangerous section of river, apprehension is overruled by self-confidence gleaned from past experience accompanied by a good jolt of adrenalin.

A few years ago I was piloting my riverboat through a long, difficult stretch of the Finlay River about twenty-five miles south of Fort Ware. This section of the Finlay braids out in numerous channels and many of the channels are choked by dangerous drift piles. On several occasions I was forced to steer my boat through narrow openings of water and directly in front of these piles. One slip or a motor failure would result in my thirty-six-foot boat being turned into kindling or rolled under a log jam. When I had finally passed the last of the bad water, I beached the boat on a sand bar for a short rest and a smoke to settle my nerves.

Not long after I had stopped a riverboat appeared coming down the river. On board were four Native fellows from Ft. Ware. These men were on their way to Ingenika to visit relatives. They would be traveling back up the river later that day. They would have to pass through the dangerous sections twice, just to pay a social call! They took the danger in stride as an everyday occurrence. These were rivermen.

Trapping—After the War

When World War II broke out, many of the men from the river country joined up, just as they did all across Canada. The provincial government required the owner of a registered trapline to use it or lose it. The province collected not only a trapping license fee but also a royalty that was levied on each animal caught. An exemption was made for any trapper that enlisted; his trapline would be kept for him until he returned.

When Buck Buchanan and his wife Elsie made that epic winter trip in 1930, their children Jean, age six, and Frank, age eight, accompanied them. Frank grew up helping his dad on the trapline and running a trading post throughout the 1930s. When World War II broke out, Frank joined up and got into action overseas. He was among the lucky soldiers that returned home after the war with his carcass intact. He headed north and joined his dad on the traplines. They trapped the Wicked River country in 1946. It was here on the Peace River where Frank came closer to death than at any time during his war years.

Frank was traveling on foot down the frozen Peace River heading to one of his line cabins. His dad was about an hour behind him. Frank was carrying the usual backpack of traps and bait as well as about ten pounds of potatoes.

The big rivers of the north never freeze evenly. The sides harden up first with the middle, where the faster current is, freezing last. During periods of mild weather the fast-flowing water underneath can reopen sections of the river. When colder weather again refreezes these sections, the ice may only be a few inches thick when a light snow fall covers the deadly trap. Frank was crossing the river when, without warning, the ice gave way and in he went. His parka trapped some air against his body and kept him afloat from the armpits up. His pack fell off but his snowshoes, still on his feet, were catching the river current and began to pull him downstream. He kept breaking the thin ice with his

elbows ahead of him in an effort to keep from being pulled under. After he had drifted about seventy feet the ice became thicker and he could not break it anymore; he was now chest deep in ice cold water and hanging on with both arms extended out in front on the ice shelf. His legs were being pulled downstream by the snowshoes. He was in a desperate situation.

At this point Frank knew he must act, do something, or the cold water would soon take its toll and he would be a goner. Very slowly he placed one arm under the ice and pushed up. He now had a kind of bear hug on the ice shelf, carefully he then drew one leg back against the current and was able to roll it up onto the top. His strength was fading fast, but with a final effort he was able to roll his whole body up onto the ice. He dared not stand yet or he might break this thin ice again, so he rolled along until he felt he was on solid ice. He now faced a new danger; it was -20°F with a strong wind. He would soon freeze to death in his wet clothes. The snowshoes that had nearly killed him, now saved his life. It was two miles to the cabin over deep snow. He never would have made it without those snowshoes. He got to the cabin and was soon warming up by the stove. He never even got frostbit.

When his father came downriver an hour later, Buck's heart nearly stopped when he saw his son's tracks go into that black hole, but his hopes leaped when he found the tracks again farther along. He told Frank later that he had checked under every spruce tree expecting to see Frank over a fire and was surprised that Frank went straight for the cabin.

During his years in the north as a trapper, Frank learned a lot about the animals he trapped. To be successful a trapper has to think like the animals he's hunting to anticipate their next move. A trapper named Eklunt from the Ospika River country had told Frank that certain wolverine lived to a great age—thirty years or more. Frank saw the evidence of this himself.

His dad, Buck, had not trapped a certain creek drainage for twenty-two years. Frank decided to lay a string of traps in this area the next winter but first walked up the valley in the spring of the year to check it out. A wolverine will often circle a trap set or any disturbance by man after he learns to associate it with food. There had been no human activity for more than twenty years in this area. Frank was following old blaze marks on the trees that marked the faint trail up the valley. A wolverine had passed up the valley just a day before him and the animal's tracks were clearly visible in the snow. At every blazed tree the wolverine did a complete circle! Had this animal remembered, from twenty years past, that he used to get a meal at these locations?

The cold is an ever-present danger to trappers and Joe Berghammer was not as fortunate as Frank Buchanan. Joe, "Hamburger Joe" as he was known throughout the river country, had come into the area to prospect and trap. His cabin was located near Deserters Canyon. During one extreme cold spell the temperature dropped to forty below and Joe had somehow gotten his feet wet and froze all the toes on one foot. As he sat in his cabin thawing out, his toes began to blacken and blister. After a few days he knew he was in trouble as gangrene set in. Every woodsman knows there is only one way to save your life in this situation—amputate. The first thing Joe did was partially refreeze

"Hamburger" Joe Berghammer with George New operating the boat, Parsnip River, 1940.   *Photo: Carl New*

his foot to kill the pain of the operation. He cut around each toe at the base and pulled back the skin. He then took a cold chisel and hammer and chiseled off his toes one at a time. When this gruesome task was finished, he rolled the skin back over the stubs and sewed each one up, finishing the job by pouring a little rum over the foot. A lesser man would probably have passed out in the middle of the operation. Joe's ordeal wasn't over yet.

He had to keep himself warm for the weeks of recovery he faced and that meant keeping his fire stoked with wood from the shed fifty feet from his cabin. His good foot was still recuperating from mild frostbite as well, and of course he could put no weight at all on the amputated one. Laying on his back and using his elbows, Joe wormed his way out to the woodpile. He then piled a small stack of wood on his stomach and elbowed his way back to the cabin on his back! By spring Hamburger Joe was fully recovered and in perfect health.

Joe was a prankster but didn't like it when the tables were turned on him. On occasion he was known to bump a man as he stood on a dock or gangway, and into the river the hapless man

would go. Joe once was having a friendly wrestling match with a man who weighed only 140 pounds. He was trying to throw the smaller man into the Finlay but underestimated the other man's strength and Joe was pitched in instead. Joe stomped off in a huff.

Another test of strength, this time with the tough Irishman Ben Corke, turned a little rough and Joe gave the older man his best punch right in the midsection. He missed the mark and hit Ben in the hip instead. Ben happened to be carrying a big emery stone in his hip pocket and Joe hit it square on. The fight ended with Joe running around yelping with a sore fist.

The company a man keeps can get him into trouble, as Hamburger Joe found out when traveling with Shorty Weber during the War Years. Weber was not above bending the laws. He had been a prime suspect in several serious crimes. The police, however, had never been able to pin Weber down.

The Ingenika Mine had been mothballed and the caretaker was absent when Weber motored his riverboat up to the site. Gasoline was rationed during the War Years and expensive, to boot, when it was available. The two partners in crime emptied several forty-five-gallon drums of aviation gasoline belonging to the mine into their own barrels on board the riverboat. They then replaced the stolen gas with river water hoping no one would notice. They noticed! This time the police caught Weber and Joe red-handed and shipped the culprits out for trial. Both men were of German ancestry and their nationality was held against them— Canada being at war with Germany. Not only were Joe and Weber convicted of theft but also the more serious charge of sabotage. Two years in the crow bar hotel was the punishment.

When Joe began to get long in the tooth he moved into Prince George and got a bit of work at Williams Store, and he lived above the store in a small room. He liked to play practical jokes on the store staff and was always clowning around with them. Mrs. Williams and some of the other women put a dozen loose eggs down in his sleeping bag one evening. As Joe slid into his bag that night, things got a little slimy. Revenge for the ladies was sweet.

When Joe Berghammer was an old man, he had an attack of appendicitis. He needed an operation, but because of his age, the doctors sent him down to Vancouver where there was better care in case of complications. Old Joe was lying in bed as the doctor examined him. His feet were hanging over the end of the bed and the doctor noticed the stub of a foot. "What happened to your foot?" he asked Joe.

"I chopped my toes off. What do you think happened?" replied the cantankerous old trapper. The doctor was so amazed when he heard Joe's story that he had all the interns at Vancouver General Hospital come by Hamburger Joe's bed for a look.

Grizzly bears were a menace on the lines, and any trapper who had spent time in the north country usually had a close call with the big bear sometime in his career.

The grizzly seemed to appear out of nowhere in the tall grass. It was up on its hind legs for a better look at his prey, that being a trapper named Ken Christopher. Ken was carrying a heavy pack of traps and beaver pelts across the wide Police Meadows that ran off the Finlay River just north of Fort Graham. With a roar the big

boar charged, Ken shucked his pack and levered a round into the .30-30 Winchester he was carrying. Knowing a grizzly will often run a bluff charge, Ken roared back at the oncoming bear and stood his ground with the rifle at his shoulder. The bruin suddenly turned ninety degrees and ran into the trees seventy yards back of Ken. The bear was gone—or was he? Ken had learned a thing or two since he had come into the river country with his stepfather Ben Corke in 1938, and one thing was to never trust the big bears. Shouldering the backpack again, he carried on out across the meadow. A sixth sense told him to look over his shoulder, and sure enough the bear was back. This time the grizzly meant business, no roar, just a flat-out charge with head low and ears laid back. Ken knew he was underarmed for grizzly but remembered what Ben had taught him—make the first shot count. That meant waiting until the bear was almost on him, not an easy thing to do with 800 pounds of homicidal fury coming at you. Ken waited for that bear. He held the sights just below the open jaw and shot the bear through the neck at ten paces. The grizzly dropped as if pole-axed. All in a day's work on the trapline? Well not exactly. Ken sat on his pack to roll a smoke and collect his nerves. "I tore up three cigarette papers trying to roll that smoke," he told me, "and that was with my elbows resting on my knees."

Carl New had only trapped a couple of years when WW II broke out and he enlisted in the Canadian Army. While helping liberate Belgium from the Nazis, Carl met a young woman from Antwerp named Emily and, like day follows night, they fell in love and married. Carl returned to Canada with his war bride. In the fall of 1946, the two of them went to his Anzac River trapline for the winter trapping season. Emily wasn't so sure about this game plan; it was all a new experience for her.

Their first hard day on the river ended with the newlyweds spending the night under canvas at Davie Lake. "I'm not going to sleep in that flimsy tent with bears around," Emily said.

"There's no bears around here," Carl replied.

Emily was skeptical but finally relented and they spent an uneventful night. They loaded up the riverboat first thing in the morning and Carl had motored a little way down Davie Lake when a bear appeared on the beach. Emily was not impressed.

Her adventures were not over yet, however. As winter progressed she had to learn to use snowshoes and do her best to keep up with Carl. On one occasion, Carl decided they would both spend the night in the furthest of his line cabins. This would be Emily's first trip to this remote section of the line. Every trapper has names for each of his cabins and this one was called the Dead Man's cabin.

"Dead Man's cabin?" asked Emily.

Carl told her the body of a trapper who died of an unknown cause was buried under the porch steps. There had been three people working the trapline and only one made it out alive. The whereabouts of the second dead man was never determined. Scurvy was probably the cause of death for both men. Police investigations were often not done in the earliest part of the cen-

WENDY WOOD cci

tury. A survivor's statement was often taken at face value and due to the remoteness of the traplines, a follow up by police was impossible.

That spring Carl was taking the riverboat, with Emily aboard, up the Anzac River when a huge ice floe appeared bearing down on them. Carl tried to do a U-turn to get back downriver and out of harm's way. His long boat, with Emily at the bow, didn't quite make the turn on the narrow river and the bow drove into some willow bushes growing in the water. Emily instinctively grabbed the first bush and for some reason didn't let go. She was pulled out of the boat. Luckily there was a horizontal log snag sticking out from shore into the river and she managed to scramble up on this. The riverboat with only Carl in it was swept downstream, but Carl motored back up to rescue his stranded wife.

Emily was a plucky lady and she survived that first year on the trapline and even returned the following year to help Carl build a bigger home cabin.

The trappers tried to look out for one another as much as possible, but the nature of the job meant long periods of isolation and no immediate help in emergencies. A young trapper named Gunnar Loveng took over trapping on Frank Buchanan's line one season and met with tragedy. Often times a man was not missed until the spring breakup when he was due out after the winter's trapping to sell his fur. Loveng never showed up at Finlay Forks from his line fourteen miles down the Peace River. Dick Corless reported him missing first and a search was begun in June. The RCMP, with Frank's help, could find no trace of Gunnar or his dog. The Peace keeps a lot of secrets down in its cold depths.

Johnson (first name unknown) was a longtime trapper from the Finlay Forks area. His line was up the Manson River. In 1948 this trapper failed to rendezvous in Finlay Forks at his usual time and a police search party was sent out. The police located a site where Johnson had killed a caribou. The trapper had made one trip with a packboard of meat to his cabin and then returned for another load. He never made it back with that second load. A grizzly had laid claim to the caribou and killed Johnson from ambush. The bear, uncharacteristically, carried off the trapper and left part of the caribou behind. The searchers could see all this from the signs left in the snow but were unable to find any trace of the victim. Undoubtably, the grizzly devoured the man. His dog was still tied up back at his cabin but was in such condition from starvation the police had to shoot him.

In about 1935 Jack Weisner froze his feet while up in the Gataga River country 100 miles north of Fort Ware. He was immobilized so long that his grub supply ran low and Weisner got so desperate that he ate one of his dogs. He nearly burned his cabin down after accidentally knocking over a kerosene lantern during his ordeal and was quoted later as saying, "I was at the point of shooting myself."

A passing trapper named Jack Blanchard found Weisner in a bad state and knew he had to get the stricken man out to a doctor fast. This was no mean feat when the nearest professional was 250 miles away in Hudson Hope. A remarkable journey ensued that involved the cooperation of several men. Blanchard and some Natives strapped Weisner on a dogsled and took the trapper as far as Fort Ware. At this point, trappers Don Miller and Art Blair transported him on a hand toboggan down to Finlay Forks. Their route was down the ice of the Finlay River, but when they came to Deserters Canyon they encountered open water. The two men had to portage the prostrate Weisner over the steep trail around the canyon. Weisner was not a good patient. He grumbled constantly and even though there was nothing wrong with his hands, he insisted the men roll his cigarettes for him. On the steep descent of the trail, Miller was lowering Weisner down the hillside by rope, with Blair down below on the flat to receive the toboggan. Miller ran out of rope and hollered below to Blair, "What should I do now?"

Blair shouted back, "Let the miserable old bugger go," and Miller did just that. Weisner went bumping down the trail and the sled shot out onto the river ice.

At Finlay Forks the relay continued on with Jim Van Somer and the game warden Vic Williams taking over. Seventy miles later these good Samaritans reached Jim Beattie's place on the Peace River and Jim took Weisner overland by horse and sleigh into Hudson Hope. Remarkably, Weisner only lost two toes in the ordeal.

Wendy Liddle, cgi

The bone-chilling cold of midwinter is a constant companion for the men who worked the trails for their living. Ernest Erickson, a trapper from Summit Lake, had missed his ride from Prince George to Summit Lake. In 1931 there was not a lot of traffic on the rough dirt road north of town, especially at night, so Ernest set out walking for home in -35°F weather. (The twenty-six miles distance was not too far for a young man in good shape.) Around 3:00 A.M. his brother Wilfred heard a noise on the porch of his cabin at Summit Lake. It was Ernie. "Help me get my boots off," he ordered his younger brother, "I think my feet are frozen." When Wilfred pulled off the boots and socks, all Ernie's toenails came with them. Ernie's feet survived, however, and eventually the toenails grew back.

Roland Skog was no riverman, and he'd have been the first to admit it. A good trapper yes—but, unlike most other trappers, Skog did not like the water at all. One spring day in 1946 at Summit Lake, he was loading up about 400 pounds of supplies into his twelve-foot rowboat for the trip down the Crooked, Pack and Parsnip Rivers to his cabin near Weston Creek. The Crooked was in full flood and with the high water the river's many riffles were now considerably more dangerous. Roland was nervous about the trip. Al Huble happened to be headed down river himself with a big riverboat. He asked Roland if he would like him to take his supplies down for him. Roland jumped at the chance but said he would take the empty row boat down himself, as Al's boat was now pretty well loaded. Huble left ahead of Skog and unloaded the trapper's supplies at the Lone Tree cabin below the worst of the rapids. Skog eventually arrived too, but not before flipping his small boat over in Cottonwood Riffle.

Skog was described as a lonely man, but he seemed to prefer his solitary life at the Parsnip River cabin. He was self-educated and maintained a large library of books in his cabin. He was also an avid astronomer. In fact, he owned various telescopes to watch the night sky. He was an excellent carpenter and built his own birch furniture. The rivermen would stop for coffee at his place on occasion and everyone liked this interesting man.

Skog owned a huge malamute-husky cross sled dog. This animal could stand on his hind legs with his front paws on Skog's shoulders and look the trapper in the eye. Wolves had been howling nightly around Skog's cabin one winter and one morning, just as Roland untied his dog for a run, two of the wild canids appeared below the cabin out on the ice on the Parsnip River. The big husky immediately ran out after the wolves to scare them off. They didn't scare! When the dog was still forty yards away, the wolves turned the table and came snarling at the dog. The husky swapped ends and ran for his life with the two wolves hot on his tail. Roland Skog meanwhile had gotten his rifle loaded and was standing on the porch as his husky shot past and ran into the cabin. One of the wolves nearly bowled Skog over trying to get at the dog and almost ran into the cabin too before realizing its mistake. Skog regained his composure enough to shoot both wolves before any harm was done.

Alas, Roland Skog met an untimely end and it wasn't the river that got him. Skog was in his seventies and neither his strength nor his hearing was what it once had been.

Like most trappers, Skog had an underground root cellar dug in behind his cabin. One evening just after dark, he lit his "bitch light"—a tin can with a candle inside and a wire loop for a handle—also called a bushman's flashlight. Skog walked to his root cellar forty yards behind the cabin and loaded up a sack with potatoes. As he was carrying this load back down the trail, he failed to hear an animal sneak up on him. A grizzly bear ambushed the unfortunate fellow and with one tremendous blow killed him instantly. By the time the police arrived on the scene, the victim had been almost entirely devoured by the animal.

The grizzly bear is always a potential threat on the trapline. This animal grows to 700 pounds and some big males are larger. The bear's disposition is completely unpredictable and this is what makes it so dangerous. Wilfred Erickson knew this only too well, and avoided grizzly as much as possible. Wilfred and his brother Ernest trapped the Summit Lake area back in the 1930s and in fact Wilf still traps to this day (1997). In the early years a grizzly incident occurred that could have been deadly for Wilfred. He was trapping in early winter near where Swamp River drains into the Crooked. There was already more than four feet of snow on the ground that December and the big bears should have been hibernating then. Erickson was snowshoeing along with his young Labrador retriever just ahead of him on the trail. When they came into a little opening in the forest, the dog suddenly stopped, growled and backed up to Wilf. Only a dozen steps away a grizzly rose up and stood over a dead moose. There is only one thing more dangerous than a grizzly with a cub and that is a grizzly on his kill; he will defend it with a vengeance. With knees shaking, Wilf slowly pulled his .303 Savage rifle off his shoulder. The bear was momentarily confused but would charge any second. Moving without any sudden motion Wilf shouldered the weapon and fired at the bear's chest; immediately the dog leaped at the bear. Erickson used this diversion to leap off the trail behind some trees. The bear ignored the yapping dog and began to tear up small trees with his claws and teeth, roaring savagely as he did so. Luckily for the trapper the dog did not draw the bear back to him. The grizzly then ran off a short distance and expired in a willow patch fifty yards away.

Scurvy was another real danger on the remote traplines and this disease could render a man helpless to the point where he couldn't even keep a fire going. When the Witter boys, Hank and Bill, first came to their Philips Creek trapping country in 1923 they brought along their father, Hamilton. An Indian told the men to watch out for the black death and told them how to avert this ailment. By late March old Hamilton didn't feel so good and some of his teeth had fallen out. He was not a man to complain and kept his problems to himself. When he got to the point where even walking was painful, his son Bill knew something was very wrong. When Bill pulled up his Dad's pant leg sure enough his lower legs were going black—scurvy! Recalling what the Indian had told them, they boiled up a pot of spruce boughs and all three men drank this vile concoction. Within a week Hamilton was back to normal.

The Witters continued to trap and prospect around Philips and Lignite Creek for many years. Bill and Hank were sure they would strike it rich if they could just get at the gold at the base of a waterfall on Philips Creek and to that end they diverted the creek away from the falls. This considerable job took a few summers of hard labor but never paid off as expected. At another location, using picks, shovels and a homemade wheelbarrow, they dug a trench where they suspected gold. By the time they gave up, the ditch was eight feet high by ten feet wide and 500 yards long! The prospectors never did hit it big and their best day only netted $26. The present-day Mount Mulligan Mine is very close to where the Witters had worked and is rich in gold. Hank was an old man when his son Jerry mentioned the fact that the big strike was 300 feet below the surface. Hank said, "Hell, if Bill and I had known that we would have dug a hole down there to get it."

Hank Witter eventually married Margaret Van Somer, and not long after the marriage he asked Margaret if she would accompany him on the trapline for the coming winter season. Hank, like most trappers, used the beaver scent sacs, or castors, as his main attractant when setting traps for beaver. These glands have a very powerful smell. Margaret replied, "Hank, I'll go with you and stay all winter on one condition. You take those stinking castors out of your pockets!"

Hank retired from the bush by 1950, but his old bachelor brother Bill carried on. During the winter of 1952 a local pilot who had the mail run to Fort Ware was asked by Hank to keep an eye out for Bill on the trapline. The pilot reported that there was smoke from Bill's cabin but no snowshoe tracks around the place. On the next flight over, a few weeks later, the pilot again noticed smoke from the chimney but no tracks about. Hank was worried. He decided, in late January, to hire a helicopter and fly in to check on old Bill. As he approached the snowbound cabin, he noticed smoke from the stack and when he opened the door there was Bill laying on his bunk reading a book. "What the heck are you doing here?" he asked. Hank's suspicions were right. Bill had cut his leg badly with an ax and it was all bandaged up. Bill was just able to hobble to his wood pile stacked on the porch and luckily had a hind quarter of moose meat close at hand to stave off starvation.

Milt Warren trapped the Nation and Blackwater River areas for a few years before joining the B.C. game branch in 1949. He became game warden as well as predator control officer. A predator control officer was responsible for dealing with wolves and bears that threatened man or livestock. His duties often included the poisoning of wolves when their numbers got too high. On one assignment he had the unpleasant task of finding a missing trapper after the provincial police lost the trail. Milt was able to follow bush sign and eventually located the trapper's cabin. The man had been dead for six months and Warren had to take out the putrid corpse for autopsy.

Milt was out on predator control once when he took on the biggest adversary of his career, and it wasn't a wolf or bear. Milt was north of Summit Lake in 1950 traveling the recently completed Hart Highway. He was checking a moose carcass that he had laced with strychnine for wolf control when he noticed another fresh moose kill about a quarter mile off the road; the animal had been shot. The snow was deep this late in the winter and a clear snowshoe trail led to the moose. Someone had poached a moose out of season. An American army convoy had passed through this area on their way up to Alaska and in fact were camped only a short way up the road. Milt Warren had a fair idea someone from the convoy had shot the moose and carried part of the animal back to camp. Milt called for backup and with fellow game officer Alf Janks along, the two men confronted the United States Army. At first the commander refused the game wardens entry into the camp but relented when he was reminded that while on Canadian soil he was required to abide by Canadian law.

Evidence was found and various wildlife charges were laid against the commander. The leader's trouble multiplied however when he returned to the United States. The Canadian Federal External Affairs Department lodged a formal complaint with the United States Embassy. It seems that when a foreign army gets permission to cross Canadian soil all ammunition must be in bond, that is locked up until they leave the country. Obviously some ammunition was available to shoot the moose. A court-martial ensued and the commander was stripped of rank.

As predator control officer, Milt Warren's job entailed poisoning wolves. While performing this duty in 1954, an event took place that could have been a disaster. Milt had purchased a broken-down horse to use as wolf bait. He shot the horse, partially skinned it and then quartered the animal for easy handling. It was going to be a few days before he would be transporting the carcass to the bush, so Milt arranged with Slim Cowart, a retired trapper, to leave it hanging in Slim's shed located on the outskirts of Prince George. Milt made the serious mistake of lacing the horse meat with strychnine in advance of placing it in the field. The meat was stolen from the shed!

The thief was known to Slim Cowart and probably watched Slim and Milt as they stored the meat. Milt was frantic. If any human ingested that strychnine, he was a dead duck! The game warden figured out who the thief was and questioned the man at his cabin. The culprit however, had been smart enough to cache the meat under the snow. And, of course, denied any involvement. Before a week had passed, neighborhood dogs had sniffed out the cache and twenty pets died before Milt discovered the rest of the poisoned meat.

When winter closed in on the river country it was common practice for some white trappers to take Indian "wives" for the long season ahead. These men apparently thought the Native women were good enough as bed partners, but not good enough to take out to civilization. The derogatory term "squaw man" was used in this era to describe these men. A few of the rivermen, to their credit, came to love their women and, despite the unspoken prejudice of the time, took them out to Prince George for a proper marriage ceremony. The Catholic Church took matters into their own hands one summer and sent out a priest by riverboat. The preacher performed six marriage ceremonies right in the trappers' cabins. Although it is unclear as to how these pressured marriages turned out, the priest was determined to make honest people of them all.

The trapping of wild fur-bearing animals continues to this day. There are currently about 5,000 active trappers in B.C. and trapping is still an important industry for the Natives and non-Natives living in remote areas across Canada's north. A solitary snowshoe trail across a frozen northern lake and smoke rising from a wilderness cabin on a cold winter morning are still common sights in the river country of northern B.C.

Professional Guiding and Outfitting

As the riverboat idled into the dead water of the back sny, the big bull moose appeared, standing in the shallows. He stood and looked dumbfounded at the hunters and the boat bearing down on him; then before the guide could stop the boat, the moose took off at a run for the timber. One of the hunters took a quick shot at the departing animal. Immediately the bull turned to look at his tormentors, snorted loudly with mucus flying out both nostrils, and charged the boat. The astonished hunters now proceeded to empty their rifles at the oncoming animal, but in their panic fired wildly into the air. Ken Christopher, the guide, had to act fast, and picking up his .30-30 Winchester that was leaning against the gunnels, he levered in a round and killed the charging animal with a neck shot at thirty yards! None of the men had ever seen a moose so determined in his charge.

Early outfitters working on the Peace River, 1926. Left to right, Matt Headly and Mr. Headly Sr. In the stern of the riverboat are Jack Adams and Jim Beattie.

Photo: Bob Beattie

The moose now had to be gutted and skinned out. While doing this chore, Ken discovered where that first bullet had hit. The moose's testicles had been completely shot off! That may have explained why the moose had become so enraged. The two hunters were embarrassed about their shooting, using their high-powered expensive rifles and looked with awe at the guide's small rifle.

The business of guiding sportsmen and others on the river was exciting and at times dangerous work. The clients were usually unknown to the guide beforehand, and when the unexpected happened the guide very often had to bail a client out of trouble. This was a big responsibility. Even on river trips that were for sightseeing and picture taking only, the guide had to always be thinking ahead, anticipating problems before they arose.

Harry Philips was perhaps the earliest guide on the rivers of the Rocky Mountain Trench to be paid for his services. He owned two thirty-two-foot riverboats in the early 1920s and took tourists on trips from Summit Lake all the way to the Peace country. His clients were mostly well-heeled adventurers from the eastern United States. Curly Philips built these outboard-powered boats for his brother Harry. The design was the forerunner of, and not unlike, the product built a decade later by Jack Duncan and Dick Corless.

In 1942, a businessman and Prince George pioneer named Ted Williams asked Dick Corless to take him along when making the freight run from Summit Lake to Fort Ware. Ted was an old friend of Corless' and would help with the freight loading to more than pay his way. Williams was an avid historian and photographer. He took sixteen-millimeter movies of this trip and of another he took in 1947. These old movies were probably the first action pictures taken of the riverboats, the rivermen and the scenic mountain country of the Northern Rockies.

Pen Powell, the Charlie Lake pioneer riverman and later bush pilot, guided American sportsmen in 1942. At the time there were more than 5,000 U.S. Army troops stationed around Fort St. John and when their furloughs came around they were looking for fun. Powell built a forty-eight-foot riverboat capable of carrying

Early river guide Harry Philips with New York clients, 1929.

twenty men. He would take them at $20 per head for five-day excursions up the scenic Peace River to Finlay Forks. The soldiers would fish and hunt and take lots of photos to send back home. Powell supplied everything and built cabins for his clients at Gold Bar and Clearwater. The fishing was terrific, especially to many of the soldiers who were city boys. However, guiding sportsmen for big game never got started seriously until after World War II. Some of the rivermen took up the business as a way of picking up extra income during the fall months; Dick Corless, Jim Van Somer, Al Huble and others all took out hunters.

In the 1940s there were three classifications of guides: A, B and C. Class C could only guide a person for game birds and fish. The class A guide was the best qualified position and it was only for those who had three years guiding experience and owned suitable equipment for outfitting. The class B guide was basically working off his three-year apprenticeship to get a class A.

In 1946, Del Miller of Fort Ware held a guiding license that only cost him a few dollars. Today it would cost him $405. The nonresident hunter also got a real deal in 1946. His general firearms and anglers license cost only $25 and entitled him to take all big or small game and fish. He did have to pay a trophy fee to the provincial government of $25 per big game animal, but only after he was successful. Around the Fort Ware area moose, black and grizzly bear, mountain goat, mountain sheep and caribou could be found, so at $25 each the total cost would have been $175. Today that same sportsman would pay more than $1,700 and this would be due in advance of his hunt. The hunting regulations in 1946 were written in a small pamphlet that could be read in a few minutes; today the hunting synopsis is a confusing, ninety-page book that requires the skill of a lawyer to figure it out—times change.

As the decade of the prosperous 1950s came, wealthy Americans encouraged some of the rivermen to take up guiding in a big way. A Native by the name of Sam Chingee was a class A guide for a number of years on the lower Parsnip River and to this day the Chingee family from McLeod Lake employs many each fall, taking out hunters for moose, black bear and grizzly bear. Sam and his brothers Harry and Alex started to hunt and fish at an early age. Their elders would take the young boys up to the alpine meadows to shoot "whistlers" or marmots. After dressing the animal it was placed over an open fire to singe the hair off and then roasted.

The Chingee brothers would work the Parsnip, Misinchinka, Pack and Crooked Rivers looking for game for their American clients. Navigating the narrow Misinchinka required a skilled river rat. The first six miles of this river are continuous riffles with many tight bends. To compound the difficulty, there are deadly drift piles to negotiate around. The Crooked River was phenomenal for moose. In the fall of the year a migration would occur with hundreds of moose moving from the Rocky Mountains down to the willow flats of the Crooked for winter. On one trip from McLeod Lake to Summit Lake fifty-six different moose were counted. Once during the moose rut, Sam Chingee heard more than twenty different moose grunting around Scovels Bar on the Parsnip. Grizzly bears were also numerous. These were the big bush grizzlies, weighing up to 600 pounds and, like today, the grizzly could be trouble.

When a person has a strong aversion to doing something, an old saying is, "I'd sooner slow dance with a cranky grizzly." Harry Chingee almost did just that! Harry and his two brothers were moose hunting for their own winter's meat. The men split up to better cover the country and Harry was following moose tracks up into some high country. Without warning, a grizzly bear broke out of the trees and came charging at him. Before Harry could get his rifle into play, the bear was almost upon him. It then did the unexpected and stopped short of its prey, with only seven feet to go! The bear now began to circle Harry and salivated as it looked him over. This was Harry's chance and he shot at the bruin with his .30-30, aiming for its head. At the shot the bear growled and ran off twenty feet into a willow-covered depression in the ground. The bear was definitely still alive and kicking. At this point Harry decided to retreat and round up his two brothers for backup. When the three men returned, sure enough the bear was still in his hole and hidden by the dense willows. The men could see a moose's leg sticking out of the bear's den and could smell the bear's strong odor. The grizzly began to growl and roar savagely; it obviously knew the hunters were near and it was not going to invite them to dinner unless they were going to be dessert. This was still a very healthy bear, so Harry's bullet must have just grazed the bear's

WENDA LIDDLE, c9°

jaw. The men now decided they really wanted to get home to pay some overdue bills and go shopping for detergent with their wives. The bear was left to enjoy his meal.

One fall hunting season on big McLeod Lake the Chingee brothers had a forgettable trip. Harry was taking out a rich American and his adult son for a moose hunt. They had earlier spotted five different bull moose around the shore late in the day but could not get close enough for a shot. First thing next morning they were back in the riverboat and moving in on one of the big moose. The elder hunter was going to show his son how to shoot. Unknown to Chingee was the fact that neither man had ever done any big-game hunting. The older hunter began to get more visibly excited the closer they got to the unsuspecting moose. Harry shut off the outboard motor and the boat drifted well within shooting range. The American moved up to the front of the boat to shoot off the bow, using it as a rest to steady his aim. As he moved ahead his rifle was pointing downward and suddenly went off, blowing a hole in the bottom of the boat. The hunter felt foolish, Harry was flabbergasted and the moose was in flight.

Ken Christopher took over Sam's guiding territory and ran it successfully for more than a decade. The episode that occurred at the beginning of this chapter took place while Ken was still working for Sam and was in fact his first experience as a big game guide. Christopher hired his uncle, Med Crotteaux, and one of the best hunters in the river country, Pete Masatow, to be his assistants. Over the years the three guides had many memorable experiences and formed lasting friendships with their hunters, several of whom came back year after year for the excellent moose hunting.

One of Ken's riverboats had an automatic bail setup. Once the boat was under way, the plug was pulled out and the venturi or suction action drained out any water that had accumulated. The trick was to always remember to replace the plug before the boat came to a stop or everything worked in reverse. A certain hunter had watched Ken use this system a few times and thought he'd be helpful one particular morning and pulled out the plug, unbeknownst to Ken. About this time a moose came into view on an island in the Finlay River. One of the two hunters shot but only wounded the animal. Ken hurriedly ran the nose of the riverboat onto shore and leaped off to pursue the wounded animal that had just disappeared into the bush. He instructed the other two men to remain on the beach and he would try to drive the moose back out into the open. The moose had not traveled very far as he had been hit hard, so Ken had no difficulty getting the animal out on the beach where one of the hunters finished him off.

The big job of cleaning and skinning took about two hours. When the three men finished they went back to the boat. What boat? The craft had sunk with only the tip of the bow visible. The hunter fessed up as to the probable cause and Christopher ordered him to strip down and climb in the water to retrieve the bow line. They slowly pulled the boat up on shore and the shivering hunter bailed it out.

There was generally a good-natured rivalry between guides. Each guide outfitter was assigned by law an exclusive territory, so there were no conflicts over the actual hunting locations themselves and this encouraged conservation by each guide. At the end of each season however, the talk would center around who had the highest success rate and who had taken the biggest antlered bulls. One particular fall the weather had been unseasonably hot and this, coupled with a late rut, was making the moose hard to find. When the weather is warm, the moose feed a lot at night and Ken's hunters hadn't even seen a moose. Each day the men would work the river from dawn to dusk, hiking back off the river to check the willow flats and backwaters. They were getting nowhere. Ken decided to do a little scouting up in some higher elevations in an attempt to locate even some sign of where all the moose had gone. He discovered a high meadow that was littered with fresh moose tracks. The abundance of moose wallows indicated that the bulls were using this spot as a rutting ground. Each bull was endeavoring to round up a harem of cows.

The next morning Ken stationed the three guides and six hunters strategically around the mile-square meadow in the hopes one or two moose would show up. They did, and in spades! It was late in the evening and getting dark before the last of the six moose had been packed out to the river's edge, and the exhausted but happy men headed up river to their camp by moonlight.

A few days later Christopher and his hunters took the moose out to the Parsnip River landing where the meat could be loaded into the trucks. Another outfitter that held the territory to the east was also unloading gear at the landing but his hunters had gotten skunked. Ken's riverboat pulled up to the dock with six big sets of bull moose antlers proudly displayed. The unlucky four looked with envy at the loaded boat, and one took Ken aside to ask if there was a chance they could book a hunt with him next autumn.

When moose populations are high, as they were in the Finlay and Parsnip valleys, the wolves are not far behind. Wolf populations can reach very high levels as long as the prey species are abundant. The wolf does not have any natural enemies with the exception of man and a deadly form of mange.

By the sound of their lonely howls, Ken could tell a big wolf pack was near his hunting lodge above Finlay Forks. It was night and Ken was worried for his old pack horse Chief. Chief's barn was about half a mile back off the river beside a natural hay meadow. All night long the pack's howling could be heard from the direction of the meadow and Ken fully expected to find his horse dead in the morning. As he approached the meadow, he could plainly see the wolf tracks in the snow. What a relief. There was old Chief with his head sticking out of the barn door. The snow around the barn was tamped flat with wolf tracks but Chief had outsmarted them. He knew the wolves would try to get behind him for their

Al Huble Jr. with hunter and grizzly bear.   *Photo: Al Huble*

attack so he backed into the small barn and faced them. None of the wolves was foolhardy enough to face those bone-crushing front hooves of the horse.

During Al Huble's years as a guide he took out numerous hunters—American, a few Europeans and one or two wealthy Canadians—for moose and bear hunts. While most of the sportsmen were enjoyable, some were barely endurable. He had one particular gentleman, whose shooting ability left a lot to be desired, out for a moose hunt. The safest place to be when he was shooting was where this guy was trying to aim. He was hunting the shoreline of a small lake when two bull moose stepped out in the open and walked a few steps into the water; the moose were about 150 yards away. Before Al's hunter could get a shot off, the moose stepped back into the bush and out of sight. It was getting late in the morning, and Al figured the moose wouldn't likely come back out as it was about the time moose normally bed down for the day. "Let's get back to the boat where our lunches are," Al said. So the men began to work their way back to the river. They had only gone a short distance when another bull moose rose up from its bed just ahead of them, not more than twenty feet away! "Let him have it," Al said to the hunter. The man's shot was wild and twigs rained down on the moose from a high shot into the tree cover ahead. The bull began to circle and the hunter shot again. He only nicked the moose this time and the animal promptly ran off. At this point the fellow wanted to run into the thick cover after the moose. "Hold it," Al said, "All you're going to do is drive that poor animal out of the country. We'll give him thirty minutes then start quietly after him." The hunter was impatient but Al stood his ground and they waited as Al watched his timepiece. When the men resumed the hunt, they found the moose only a short distance away—still standing. In his excitement the man missed twice. Al watched his man raise his rifle for a third shot and at the same time shouldered his own weapon. Al fired the instant the fellow fired and finished the bull with a neck shot. The hunter never even knew Al had shot and believes to this day that he shot the moose.

Len Pickering had been a guide for more than forty-five years and he had never seen anything like this before. The cow moose had swum the Anzac River, still in full spring flood, and was calling for her three-week-old calf to follow. As Len watched from a high bank, the moose calf, all sixty pounds of him, jumped into the boiling river in an attempt to keep up to its mother. Half way across a wave slapped the little guy in the face and that was enough to make him turn back. While the calf stood on the far shore, the cow became very agitated and started to bark loudly at the calf, scolding him and running back and forth along the shore. She obviously sensed some kind of danger. Once again the calf dove into the raging river and with its strength almost gone, it gave up this attempt also. The mother moose lost her patience and jumped back into the Anzac, swam back over to her calf, and coaxed it back into the ice cold water by biting the calf's rump. The two began to swim across side by side with the big cow on the upstream side of the calf. The exhausted calf swam for only a short way and then climbed part way up on its mother's back. The cow finished the journey by piggybacking the calf across. Just as the two animals reached the shore a large black bear appeared from out of the bush and it stood right where the calf moose had

been. The cow must have somehow known the bear was on their trail and would likely have killed her offspring.

Len Pickering owned his guiding area until he reached the age of sixty-eight in 1995, when he sold out to his son. He had many adventures over his long guiding and trapping career. He guided hunters by riverboat on forty miles of the Parsnip River and used horses in the high country. His personal hunting weapon was an old .300 Savage, small by today's standard, and claimed that he had never lost a moose with it. He guided bow hunters from the U.S. and Europe for grizzly. This was a challenging and hair-raising business at times. In fact, his outfit held the record for the largest grizzly taken with a bow and arrow for many years.

One fall, while felling a big tree for firewood, Len disturbed a denned-up black bear, a huge specimen reaching eight feet tall. He shot this one for his own eating. His wife Ruth put up more than thirty cans of rendered bear lard from this bear, enough bear grease to last more than a year.

Pickering and his sons still earn part of their livelihood by trapping in the winter, and one year they took more than 400 marten from the traplines. Len and his wife have been married for forty-eight years and today are semiretired and living near his trapping country in Bear Lake, B.C.

This guy is going to hunt moose? He not only couldn't walk, he couldn't even stand up without crutches. Never in his long career as a guide had Ken Kyllo ever come up against a hunter like this. The unfortunate Mr. Yonkey had been virtually bedridden for the past two years with arthritis and had only recently been able, with the help of modern medicines, to hobble around. As a young man he had been able to enjoy his love of the outdoors and was determined now to have at least one more hunting trip.

Kyllo and the other hunter helped the man out of the car and over to the waiting riverboat on the Parsnip River. It was late October, 1958, and this would be the Kyllo brothers' last hunting trip of the fall. Near freezing temperatures and wet weather made this last hunt somewhat of an endurance test. Kyllo was worried how this sixty-five-year-old man would hold up. Mr. Yonkey was seated on a lawn chair in the bow of the boat and Ken wrapped him in a sleeping bag. For the next few days the party would be hunting out of Ken's camp at Finlay Forks. The old fellow seemed to be enjoying himself, but a lot of stops had to be made each day for a warm up by a fire Ken would make on shore. The actual hunting was of necessity done right out of the boat and Ken hoped an easy moose would appear near the water's edge. In the end it was Yonkey's partner that shot the moose, but that did not damper his enthusiasm. He returned the next year and Kyllo guided him up to a big moose standing on shore. Yonkey, at his familiar spot in the bow, got his moose.

The Kyllo brothers, Ken and Dave, began to operate their guiding business in 1954 and their specialty was taking summer tours up the Peace River from Hudson Hope. They operated two forty-five-foot riverboats. One boat was equipped with a closed-in section with a canvas canopy that could be removed during sunny weather. The varied groups they outfitted for included the Oil Scouts of North America looking for petroleum deposits, Rotary Clubs from various western cities and even a CBC film crew for a 1957 documentary.

In the summer of 1963 Dave and Ken were engaged to take out the entire Edmonton Geographical group. This party would number fifty-three men and women. The Kyllos had four riverboats of their own and hired two more rivermen to help out as pilots. They still needed one more thirty-six-foot boat so were

133

forced to hire a local character named Jack Longstreet and his boat. Jack was, to put it mildly, lacking in the public relations area. He was a cranky old loner who would go off alone to eat and rarely talked. He was a big man and as he operated the kicker he sat on the edge of the boat. Whenever anyone stood up in his boat, or moved around, he would shout, "For Christ's sake sit down. What do you think this is, a hayrack? I'd sooner haul sh— than people." Needless to say, Dave Kyllo had to be a referee to keep the peace between his clients and Longstreet.

The logistics of feeding and housing a party this size were considerable. Tarped lean-tos had to be erected at each camp and a small eighteen-foot riverboat was sent ahead of the main party with two cooks and a bottle washer aboard. Ken Kyllo figured the geologists would like some fresh peas so had purchased unshelled peas, three sacks of them, for the cooks to prepare. This was a mistake. When the main party reached the first night's campsite, the three cooks had hardly anything prepared; they were still shelling peas!

Preparing meals for any big group is work and on the river it tends to be a rough and ready affair. BC Hydro had hired the Kyllos to take out a group of bankers to show them the potential for hydro power on the Peace River. Hydro was looking for financial backing, millions of dollars in fact, for a dam project. These men were major financiers from all over the world. One banker, a Lord Schandrin, had even been in Sir Winston Churchill's cabinet. He was shocked when he saw Dave Kyllo mixing up some potato salad for lunch, in a sooty bucket.

As much as the Kyllos enjoyed the summer excursions, it was the guiding of well-to-do sportsmen in the fall of the year that was their bread and butter. Their clients would be mostly American, and some of the hunters had spent too many years behind a desk—they were out of shape. Ken Kyllo was guiding one such man, all 300 pounds of him, for moose. There was a lookout that the guides used to spot game down in the valley, but it was a hard climb up. Ken didn't usually carry his rifle for the climb as they normally had to descend to actually hunt any game that was located. Ken mentioned to his big hunter that he too should leave the rifle behind to cut down on weight. The American decided to carry his weapon anyway, and as things turned out this decision probably saved their lives.

When Ken reached the summit his hunter was still puffing his slow way up the slope 200 yards behind him. At this point, Ken heard a moose grunt. He turned to wave his hunter up. When the man arrived he was right out of breath from the climb and excitement. Both men now used their binoculars to look for the moose below. With their attention focused on finding the animal, neither man noticed the grizzlies approaching. Suddenly Ken heard another grunt very near and looked up to see two small grizzly cubs only thirty feet away. The sow grizzly was not in sight, but Ken knew she wouldn't be far away. The cubs had spotted the men and began to hiss and spit just like house cats. All of a sudden the mother grizzly rose up out of the buck brush only twenty feet behind the cubs! The situation was deadly; Ken was unarmed and the ashen-faced hunter was frozen with fear. The grizzly, with her neck hairs bristled up, began to circle the men in an effort to get their wind. She was moving in. In an instant she would charge and be on the men in a flash. Ken hollered, "Shoot over her head! Shoot over her head!" His voice broke the trance the hunter was in and he fired. All three bears spun around and ran down out of sight. When their hearts finally slowed down the American said, "Boy Ken, I hate that."

The Kyllos often hired assistant guides to help take out clients and Harry Chipesia was rated among the best. Harry had guided up north off the Alaska Highway and was no stranger to mountains and cliffs. He gave himself a good scare one fall, however, and it required the help from the rest of the guiding crew to get him out of this jam.

Harry and his hunter made a successful stalk on a mountain goat. This billy goat had horns that could make the record book—a real "wall hanger." When the hunter shot, instead of falling, the goat walked off over a ridge and out of sight. Harry was sure the shooter had done his job and the goat was hit well. They searched all afternoon for the animal but to no avail. The men finally had to give up the search in order to descend the mountain while there was still enough light. The hunter never gave up hope however, and he spent all his spare time while in camp glassing the mountain where the goat had disappeared. His perseverance paid off; he located a motionless goat lying in front of a cave. Even though it had been three days since he last saw the billy, he was sure it was the same animal.

The next morning Harry and his hunter started their climb for the cave several thousand feet above camp. When they were about a quarter mile from the cave, Harry went on alone as the hunter thought the cliff was too steep and dangerous without climbing gear. Harry, being used to this type of terrain, soldiered on. He reached the cave mouth with great difficulty but was rewarded for his effort. There laying down was a stone-cold dead goat. Harry let out a whoop and yelled to his hunter below that he was going to roll the animal down to him. The dead animal shot down the smooth rock face and came to rest against some loose shale and balsam trees. Then Harry had a good look at this same cliff he had just climbed. He got a sick feeling in his stomach and knew he was in trouble. "There's no way I'm climbing down this mountain," he shouted to his hunter.

Back at camp the hunter reconnoitered with the Kyllos and a rescue party was assembled. Using ropes and a different route, they finally got the shaky-kneed Harry down to safety. That goat? It was definitely worth all the trouble as it took the top prize trophy for British Columbia.

Guiding wealthy sportsmen for big game came into its own primarily after World War II. This new and often lucrative occupation could not have come at a better time. In 1947, the price paid by international fur buyers plunged. Many of the local fur buyers went out of business and the Hudson's Bay Company was forced to shut down their trading post at Fort Graham. As most of the early guides were also trappers, the guiding industry took up a lot of the slack in the economy. British Columbia enjoys a vigorous guiding industry to this day, and part of the credit for this prosperous business must go to the trail-blazing guides of the past.

The Miners

The Dirty Thirties were a time of intense gold-seeking activity on the upper Peace River. When there was no employment in the towns, prospecting, even if not very successful, was at least a chance to experience some adventure. It was said that every sandbar from Finlay Forks to the Peace Canyon had a prospector working it. These men would hire the rivermen to take them up the Peace. Jim Beattie and his wife Elizabeth had a homestead at Gold Bar, located about thirty miles west of present-day Hudson Hope, and had cut out the first portage road over the big rapids of the Peace Canyon. Jim would haul the miner's boats and possessions over the trail. He was an excellent riverboat operator himself. His home was always open for the river travelers.

The miner Mort Tear and his partners Jack Blanchard, Dan Miner and Ed Short worked an underground mine thirty miles up the Pesika River (formerly Wedge River). Like that of many miners, their hard work paid only marginal returns. The trail up the Pesika to the mine crossed the river many times and was hard going all the way.

In June of 1942 Ted Williams, a businessman from Prince George, was dropped off at the mouth of the Pesika by Dick Corless. He walked into Tear's old mine not realizing how tough the going would be. The mine itself was 1,900 feet above the Pesika. He wrote in his travel journal of being wet all the time as there was, "a lot of fording the Pesika branches, all in full flood." His trip in and back to the Finlay River took longer than expected. As a result he missed his rendezvous with the Corless riverboat. The exhausted man was now faced with a forty-mile hike to Fort Graham where he hoped to catch the Hudson Bay Company inspection plane that was due in. He missed it by fifteen minutes. The weary traveler now had to build a rough raft to continue south to Finlay Forks. The fort's factor, Jack McGuire, helped him out on the project and he was soon on his way again. The seventy-mile trip took several days, with his unruly craft getting stuck on sandbars and drift piles. Ted writes, "have eaten last of summer sausages, Lipton's noodle soup and tea, a long summer." At Olson Creek he found a sunken twenty-eight-foot riverboat in a back eddy. This was jury-rigged with temporary patches back into ship shape and with a couple of paddles he hewed out of trees, Williams carried on in style. The tired traveler finally reach Finlay Forks and was able to bum a ride back to Summit Lake.

King Gething supplied the miners with his riverboats, hauling produce from the few farms near the Peace Canyon. He would drop the prospectors off each season and would periodically check on them. It was a credit to the man that many of the miners would trust King to freight out their gold.

Pete Toy's bar had produced good quantities of gold before the turn of the century. Pete Toy himself took an exceptional $100 per day from this bar way back in 1861; each summer throughout the 1930s other optimistic miners would set up there. This long sandbar was located a little way up from Finlay Forks on the Finlay River. One summer two German men, one accompanied by his wife, worked the coarse sand there for three months and succeeded in extracting a nice poke of gold for their efforts. Early that fall Ben Corke and his family were running their boat past the bar and stopped to chat with the two partners. One was missing. The one German and his wife lifted a tarp up to reveal the dead partner laying in the bottom of their riverboat. The couple explained that the man had drowned while swimming. Presumably the dead man's share would now go to his partner; strange how this tragedy occurred just at the end of the mining season.

The gold fields of the Omineca River were very active near Hogem in the late 1930s and some of the hopefuls traveled to that country via the Peace River, although most went by way of Fort

Sam Huble on sleigh, Billy the moose and Al Huble Sr., Summit Lake, 1924.

Photo: Al Huble

St. James and Takla Lake. The Ingenika Mine, about ten miles up that river from the Finlay, saw a lot of activity when it opened in 1921. Tons of heavy equipment were hauled up the Peace and Finlay Rivers by riverboat, scow and by the company boat the Ingenika. The scow was seventy-five feet long and Jim and Bob Beattie got the job of toting it over the portage around the Peace Canyon. The mine itself played out within a decade and a geologist was hired to sink test holes to test for further viable ore bodies. His report stated there was not enough gold to make it a paying proposition and the lack of a transportation system made extracting the considerable base metals impractical.

When the war came in 1939 there were suddenly jobs everywhere, jobs that paid far better wages than panning for gold. The bars of the Peace became quiet again but some of the miners, especially the hardy ones of Scandinavian descent, stayed on as trappers and rivermen.

The lure of gold brought miners into the river country from all over North America as well as Europe. Burchard Bower, age twenty-one, and his young partner Dale Roselle, age twenty, were typical adventurers who left their homes in Michigan to head north. Bower's meticulously kept diary gives a rare glimpse of a miner's life in the 1920s.

As they left Windsor, Ontario, their friends and family saw them off at the train station with vague and puzzled looks. The year was 1928 and the times had been good enough for the two lads to save up train fare and still have enough left over for a grub stake to last them a year of prospecting in the bush. After five days of train travel (costing $33 per man) the two budding prospectors arrived in Prince George and went to see Al Huble Sr. of Huble & Seebeck to get outfitted. Al also arranged transportation to Summit Lake for them. They somehow wrangled a deal on an old leaky riverboat. They christened the ship *Adventure* and were soon on their way drifting down the Crooked River. "Off for the wild—Hooray!" About ten miles down the Crooked they tried their luck fishing and Dale fell overboard while reaching for a trout dangling from Burchard's line. They camped that first night at Lone Tree and had a meal of fish "so hot off the pan that they slap your belly with their tails after you've swallowed them."

Everything was a new experience for the enthusiastic duo. On the third day they saw their first moose on Davie Lake. On July 16th they camped at Louis Tereshuk's place and slept on a

Louis Tereshuk with wolf in harness (behind lead dog), Crooked River, 1929.
Photo: Viola Weatherly

grizzly bear rug. (Louis trapped at Red Rocky Lake and eventually started a mink farm with wild mink he had live trapped. He had a pack of wolves attack his sled dogs one night and his best dog was killed. Louis set some traps for the wolves lest they come back. Sure enough the next morning he had a big brute caught by the paw—the leader of the pack. Louis managed to hog tie the vicious animal with the intention of forcing him to take the place of his dead dog. Eventually he tamed the beast and trained it to pull a sleigh!)

The two young men had a good visit with Louis who was a colorful man with a lot of stories to tell them. One story involved Louis' habit of standing with his thumb over the end of his rifle barrel. He was tapping the rifle on the ground as he talked one time and the rifle discharged, neatly shooting off his thumb.

On July 17 Burchard and Dale camped on Kerry Lake in a rainstorm and had to make a shelter out of bark. When they reached Fort McLeod they stopped to repair their leaky riverboat and dry out their gear. The long paddle across McLeod Lake had tired them out, so they camped for the night. A few days later on the Pack River they spent the night at a cabin and had company arrive. Two mounties with a pair of prisoners needed a roof for the night so room was made for all. One of the prisoners had frozen his foot the previous winter and was forced to cut off all his toes with a table knife; they had not healed yet. Burchard gave the injured man some first aid materials to mend his foot.

Our adventurers passed the mouth of the clear Nation River where it joins the muddy Parsnip River and marveled at the high cut banks located here with hundreds of swallow nests. "A mar-

Prospectors camp on the Manson River, 1929. Left to right, Ivor Johnson, Dale Roselle, Burchard Bower.
Photo: Jack Little

vel in bird home building with a (till the next washout) lien on them." They finally drifted into Finlay Forks twenty-two days out of Pontiac, Michigan.

Dale and Burchard stayed four days at the Forks with Harold and Ivor Johnson, two trapper/prospectors. At Ole Johnson's trading post they took out their free miner's license. This license enabled a prospector to look for gold anywhere not previously staked and to stake his own claim. This license was good for one year and cost $3.50 each. They earned their keep while at the Johnson's by cutting wood, a never-ending job in the north country. They also prepared letters to send back to their far-away homes.

On August 4th they began the work of poling their loaded boat up the Manson River. Being greenhorns, they had packed the boat too bow heavy and had to stop and shift the gear aft. Using a 150-foot long track line, one man would pull from shore while the other kept the nose of the boat in the deep water by using a pole. The numerous curves in the fast Manson River made tracking difficult as the line man had to continuously wade or be carried back and forth across from sandbar to sandbar. Soon the first log jam was reached and the real work began. The river was blocked solid for 100 yards, bank to bank, piled deep with a jumble of fallen and stranded trees. The men decided the easiest way would be to cut a trail through the bush along the shore and carry the freight around the jam. The heavy riverboat had to be winched along the ground using a block and tackle and ropes. This work took all day and the two tired men made camp that evening immediately upstream of the jam. Just before suppertime they saw their first bear about 200 yards away on a sandbar. Dale took a few shots at the bear with his .30-30, but to no avail.

The next day the men only went a short way to the next river blockage but their hopes soared when they found "color" (gold) on the nearby bar of black sand. Burchard now called the Manson "the River of Gold." This jam was tougher than the first and the men decided the easiest way was by chopping and sawing their way through; this only took six hours of back-breaking work. By their fourth day on the river, the Manson was "getting quite impassable," with little falls and riffles of several feet drop every hundred feet, so they found a permanent cabin site. Burchard and Dale would now be living under a lean-to tarp for the next two months until they could build a permanent cabin. Their building site commanded a good view up and down the river, situated as it was on a high, pine-tree-covered bench. The surrounding country looked to be good for game and this would be of utmost importance as much of their meat would be of the wild variety. Deer, moose and bear tracks were numerous and wild berries were in abundance. That evening, in fact, they saw another bear.

On August 12th, the two novice miners began work on the cabin. The structure would have to be made tight and warm for the coming cold months ahead. They would be building it out of logs, of course, and the dead trees sprinkled here and there would be cut for firewood. A cache would also have to be made up high enough to keep their food away from bears. For the next week the work commenced with the odd bit of prospecting thrown in, all the while keeping a lookout for big game. Up to now they had been eating mainly fish that were easily caught.

On one foraging trip for game disaster nearly struck Dale. He and Burchard had hiked up river to a falls about four miles from the cabin. While climbing along the edge of a cliff Dale fell thirty feet into the Manson River below. Luckily the water there was pooled and therefore deep enough to break his fall, but he received a bad lump on his head. A serious accident this far in the wilderness and away from professional help was nearly always fatal.

By the end of August the cabin work was shaping up quite well, so the young men went on an excursion down river by boat to Finlay Forks and further to Mount Selwyn. They found a great many huckleberries there and had a feast. Out of the sheer exuberance of youth they climbed the 7,500-foot peak in about four hours. They were also looking for a badly needed moose or caribou on this trip but had no luck. The return trip to their home cabin on the Manson was much easier now as they had acquired a small outboard motor from a resident of Finlay Forks.

On September 1st Dale and Burchard were eating their first moose steaks compliments of some passing Natives. Up to now they had existed on fish and a few grouse. The Natives had given them about fifteen pounds of meat and one taste was enough to steel their resolve to get a moose of their own. On September 3rd their friends and nearest neighbors (twenty miles away) Ivor and Harold Johnson gave them a big hunk from their 700-pound bear they had shot; the big game was starting to move due to cooler weather.

By mid-September the surrounding mountains had received a mantle of snow. This encouraged the two men to accelerate the cabin building. The roof was a big job with more than 150 poles needed for the laminated roof. This was covered with moss for insulation and then buckets of clay were hauled up from the river and a smooth three-inch layer of clay was applied to weatherproof the roof. Their old riverboat the *Adventurer* was pressed into service for the hauling of logs, moss and clay. "Pretty handy rig in this country—a freight boat." On September 28th the men moved into their new cabin and it felt like a castle after living in the lean-to all summer. They had a big celebration supper of trout, grouse, hot biscuits, tea and apple pie. They christened their home "Skookum Lodge."

By now the ducks were landing on the river and these were added to the larder that was still bereft of moose or bear. On a snowy morning, October 9th, their luck changed. They had hiked six miles from home to a little lake where they had seen moose before. All of a sudden a bull moose broke from cover like a black streak and both men opened fire. "We each socked him four or five times before he went down for good." Then a cow moose came into the open a hundred yards away and they wounded it. A follow up located the stricken animal and one more shot finished her. The two mighty hunters whooped for joy at their good fortune but soon realized the tremendous amount of work ahead of them. Fourteen hundred pounds of bull and a thousand pounds of cow moose had to be packed six miles back in a snowstorm! With a sixty-five-pound load of meat each, they began to pack the two hours one way to the cabin. It took almost a week of packing to get the meat and hides back to camp. The last trip they took back the antlers of the bull to place over their fireplace. "Pretty fine horns they are too, 21 points and yellow as gold and perfect from tip to tip." The men were so tired some nights they didn't bother to make supper and just flopped into bed.

Later in October the men built a porch and some simple furnishings. From the moose hide they made moccasins. They hauled the *Adventurer* out of the river so she wouldn't freeze in. By now they were seeing moose every day as the rut was still on: "Lots of moose are in the valley now—they call back and forth for their mates." With most of their work complete they had time for visiting and made several trips to Finlay Forks to visit the Johnsons. Mrs. Johnson, Ole's wife, would always give them some potatoes and homemade bread to take home. Dale and Burchard, in return, helped out by cutting firewood for the older couple. The other two Johnsons, Ivor and Harold, were trappers and offered the two boys the bounty money on any coyotes and wolves they could shoot or trap, so they became "wolfers."

145

In November the four men went on a trapping excursion westward to the Wolverine Mountains. Their first night there, camped near an alpine lake, was the first time the young men heard wolves howling. "Listened to wolves most of the night, sure is wild back here." Burchard fell through the thin ice here but managed to scramble out and Dale caught his socks on fire when he slept too close to the campfire one night. The trip lasted seven days. The trappers laid out a ninety-mile line of traps and they collected a cross-fox in a snare. The fox would be worth $50. "Some trip - had a great time but am minus two pairs of socks and my shirt is all tore to hell and my bloody moccasins are all shot but anyway we had a swell time."

Slowly the men were learning the skills of the bush but sometimes the learning process was risky. While crossing the frozen Finlay River in November on his way to pick up mail at Finlay Forks, Burchard had to turn back because of thin ice and must have had a close call. He writes, "couldn't get across on the ice and darned near drowned." He and Dale picked up a couple of snowshoe frames and webbed them with new babiche from their moose hides. Another lesson they learned was to be more careful when putting out campfires after they discovered their old one near the moose kills had gotten under the duff and burned a large area of 100 square yards. The fire had burned their meat scaffold and spoiled most of the meat they had cached there.

By November 11, the snow was falling throughout the north and it was the coming winter with its long months of cold and isolation that made a man think of far away places and loved ones left behind. Burchard was beginning to feel a tinge of this cabin fever when he writes, "Today's (November 11th) Armistice Day although I don't hear any whistles blown up here and there ain't no liquor to speak of unless it's 'spruce tea'." This is a slow time for all trappers, the wait for solid freeze up so the work can begin safely.

The meal at the end of the day was always a highlight and Dale learned how to cook roast beaver from some animals the Johnson brothers had caught. The days were getting shorter now, and at night the mice were very active in the cabin. Dale dug out a mouse trap from their supplies "to curb the rampant galloping about the old shack at night." On November 22nd the monotony was broken by the arrival of an Indian named William. He hired the two young men to pack supplies into his cabin for $10 each. Birch slats had to be made to make runners on the sleighs they would need for this job as well as future hunting expeditions.

By late November the Michigan boys were in need of another moose so they arranged to go on a hunt with their trapping buddies the Johnsons. The four men began a moose drive by spreading out and combing the country around some small lakes. Shortly after they began this drive a moose ran out in front but no one was fast enough to get a shot. Burchard decided to work alone for the rest of the available daylight and luck was with him. He was about to give up and, in fact, was back tracking to go home. He wrote, "Started back on my own track when I heard one of the boys coming up behind me so I waited. I thought it might be a moose however so I circled back against the wind and whistled. Then I saw it was a large bull listening for me, so I gave him one in the neck and he went down like a log." He fired another shot as a signal and Ivor Johnson joined him to help with the butchering. As they were working on the animal, they heard more shots—more than twenty! "Sounded like all hell had broken loose." Dale had even better luck than Burchard and had killed two moose fifty feet apart.

The four men camped at the scene that night. "Well we camped there and cut down dead spruce for firewood and skinned both moose. We made a bed of the skins and built a humdinger of a fire and roasted moose steaks, also I had a dozen hard tack biscuits with me. We had to melt snow for drinking water and it's one poor substitute. Didn't sleep much though the hides were warm and the fire blazed a dozen feet high. It's pretty chilly this time of year, about 15F below." (None of the hunters had sleeping bags.) About an hour after laying on the hides, the moose ticks began to abandon ship and bore into the men instead, further ending any thought of sleep.

By mid-December the snow lay deep across all the river country and Dale and Burchard were learning the joys of snowshoeing. They had picked up another paying job hauling supplies for the Indian again only this time the pack was further, twenty-three miles, using toboggan and snowshoes. Carrying backpacks and pushing the sleigh they left early on the morning of December 12th and bivouacked that night in the bush at 15°F below zero. The next morning they resumed the trip "stiff and sore. Arrived limping and tired at the mountain cabin and were paid $6 each and a pair of moccasins."

For Christmas day 1928 the boys had been invited to Finlay Forks and dinner at Louis Peterson's trading post. Both men had cut and shaved their six-month growth of beard and Burchard remarked he "felt naked without whiskers." Christmas morning at the Petersons and the wake up call was Merry Christmas instead of "get the hell out of bed and gulp this breakfast before I throw it out" which was Dale's usual morning greeting. The men made the rounds of the few settlers in Finlay Forks, and went skiing on Louis' new skis he had made and "lots of tumbles." They joined in a shooting match on the river, and then enjoyed a good Christmas dinner. After supper "we tobogganed and had a great time, dropped to 10°F above and a full moon, a beautiful Christmas night complete with Northern Lights. We played cards and checkers and Ivor Johnson and I took a four-mile snowshoe jaunt at 10:00 p.m. on the river bed, ate oranges, apples and candy, sure had a good time."

The boys were starved for mail. When it finally arrived on January 3, 1929, with nine letters, it was heaven. The next mail delivery would not be until Easter. The boys couldn't wait that long and preparations were made for a 250-mile return trip to Hudson Hope to check the mail. After a sourdough pancake breakfast Dale, Burchard and a friend they had met in Finlay Forks named Kent Robinson set off for Hudson Hope in the dead of winter January 9, 1929. Two men at a time took turns pulling the toboggan as they had no dogs. The snow was deep on the ice-covered Peace River and the lead man had the toughest job of breaking trail. They made the cabin at the Wicked River mouth at 1:00 P.M. and they were too tired to continue, "had a jolly supper and pipe smoke." The next day's fourteen-mile run took them to another trapper's cabin, an old one with a five-gallon gas drum for a stove that nearly smoked them out of the cabin.

The weather was turning colder and the men put on more sweaters. They made the Otter Tail River the next day and stayed in Mr. Mercer's cabin, his nickname was Purley Pa, and the old boy cracked open a bottle of rum for the cold travelers.

The trio got off to a late start on the morning of January 12th, a little hung over, but still managed the seventeen miles to Carbon Creek Jones' place. "Charley Jones welcomed us like long lost brothers of some fraternal order, likewise Mrs. Jones. Very nice people. We met John Darling, land settler near there, and Dale and I stayed in his cabin that night." The next day's destination was the Beatties' ranch, and even though Mr. Beattie was suffering from a bout of appendicitis the couple made them welcome. The young Americans were seeing the wonderful hospitality of Canadian frontier people first hand.

Jim Beattie was one of the earliest settlers in the upper Peace River country. He eventually lost the lower part of one leg because of infection, but that didn't slow him down much. Peg Leg Jim could still ride a horse well. He would sit astride his mount with the stump of the leg in a sort of homemade leather boot attached to the saddle. Someone once asked him how he could possibly ride with only one leg and he replied, "Where I can't use my leg, I use my head."

On January 14th the three men reached the Portage cabin twenty miles and 20°F below zero later. They were played out. That night it dropped a further 15° to minus 35°F and the drafty cabin was "cold as hell. Spent cold night as we had no blankets to speak of and slept in clothes."

On January 15th the travelers reached Hudson Hope after another fourteen-mile walk. The town consisted of about twenty houses perched on the flats above the 300-yard wide Peace River. Dale and Burchard picked up their mail and joined a few of the other bachelors from Hudson Hope for a little party in their honor as "long imprisoned men from the wilds." After a day of bumming around town the return trip was started on January 17th. Two days later on the wind-blown Peace River all three men suffered frost bite. Burchard and Kent both froze their nose and Dale his cheek, but with prompt attention all were okay.

The temperature was really dropping now and it was suggested by Charlie Jones and his wife that they spend a few days at their cabin until the cold snap broke. "Charlie hauls out a cask of wine and nothing to do but spend a couple of days there as he agreed it would be 45°F below on the river tomorrow, it was by gosh 62°F below through the night; the kerosene in the lamps froze up!" By the 23rd the men resumed their journey, cold or no cold, and Burchard notes, "Up early and left for Paint Creek in 50F below zero weather and bad wind - devilish cold. I fell through (the ice) but changed socks and moccasins before I froze my feet. Only made eight miles today and stopped—too cold to travel. Up and off at 9:00 a.m. Made Selwyn cabin 14 miles in a blizzard and extreme cold, 62°F below on the thermometer." By late afternoon on the 25th the worn out men finally reached Finlay Forks but Dale discovered he had left his rubbers at Selwyn Creek and had to back track "38 more miles for carelessness."

Back at their home cabin Dale and Burchard settled into a well-deserved rest period. Their quiet life was interrupted, however, on January 31st with the arrival of the Indian who had hired them earlier in the winter. "William Basil came and we put him, his dogs, and his squaw up for the night (they left us flea ridden)."

By late February their meat supply and wood pile were getting low, so Dale decided to drop a pine tree to use for firewood. Things didn't go quite as planned. Dale felled the 125-foot pine right across the front of the cabin, demolishing the porch. Burchard states, "Lucky it didn't hit three feet in or the roof would have come down on me..." The hunting wasn't going much better either, as the moose seemed to have disappeared. This forced the men to look for game in unfamiliar country.

"Hunted from 9:00 a.m. to 4:00 p.m. and had a tough time climbing over windfalls and brush up on the flats toward the Parsnip River. Vowed never to go in that country again." They did, however, find a dead calf moose in the Manson River three

WHOOPS!

miles below their cabin. "Had fallen through the ice and it was over his head. His struggling had broken ice for a twenty-foot circle but to no avail - poor little devil."

The winter had hardened up both men and on one hunt on March 12th and 13th they walked a total of forty miles in their quest for meat. By March 28th the food supply was getting seriously low. Burchard writes, "Spent day thinking of grub I'm gonna eat when I get back (U.S.A.). Our grubs damn low now." Finally on April 6th they connected on a moose although it was strong tasting from feeding on a steady winter diet of willow tips—"Moose awfully strong from poplar buds, whooee!"

In mid-April the weather was considerably warmer and both men were looking forward to getting out to civilization for a holiday. They were planning to take the first riverboat out once the river ice broke. Burchard was particularly anxious. "Wait till I hit a hotel; I'll steep in the bath tub the first night." Dale and Burchard were both suffering from a touch of scurvy due to an absence of fresh greens. "Had an attack of scurvy for last day or two and an Indian told me of spruce tea. My blood is getting better after the tea and my swollen forehead is going down." They also ate a few yeast cakes and, with the fresh moose meat, soon regained their health enough to work sluice boxes for gold. The warmer weather was also bringing out the ducks, and these along with some grouse were a welcome change in diet. The Manson River was breaking up in places and the remaining ice was very unsafe, Burchard finding this out first hand, "I crashed through some rotten ice into six feet of water - caught myself before all wet however and Dale pulled me out."

April 19th was a red letter day for moose sightings. "Had lunch and as we sat reading in the cabin door I looked up when a twig snapped and there stood three moose, seventy-five feet away across the river on the sandbar, looking at our cabin! A big bull, a cow and a yearling calf. I managed to get a snapshot picture of the bull from the doorway without making them scared, but as I sneaked around a tree to get a closer picture of the bunch they bolted and I had to let it go. Holy Moses we could have shot all three had we needed meat and right at our door...after months of toil and trudging the forest and burns and nary a sign of life, it never rains it pours."

The exuberance of youth can lead to trouble and this along with impatience brought another close call to the young adventurers. The Manson River was swollen to twice its normal size and the brown, swift water was choked with passing pans of ice; it was no place for a riverboat yet. Dale and Burchard decided to improvise a way across the river. "We decided to ferry across on a big ice cake. We broke off a big piece (from shore) twenty feet long and eight feet wide and got on and the current took us out in the middle pronto." After they managed this ungainly raft across to the other side with no problems they decided to ride her down the rapids below the camp. "In the middle of the swift water and rocks the ice pan broke in three pieces and I, being on a piece four feet square, made a jump onto a larger piece and went bumping down the stream. I was afraid she'd crack up and let me down into the rapids but she held and I managed to jump to shore below about 100 yards. Dale on his ice chunk got stuck in the center of the swift water and had to pole vault and splish through knee deep water to the shore...never again."

For the next two weeks the larder was restocked with the abundant geese and ducks that were returning from their exile down south. By May the fishing was picking up for rainbow trout, grayling and dolly varden up to ten pounds. The bear were also coming out of hibernation.

"Dale had an experience with a bear this afternoon that was a howl! He came around the edge of our cabin to get a chunk of firewood as he was cooking dinner. He rounded the corner of the cabin - head down - a big black bear crawls out of the garbage pit with a big woof! They both parted company and Dale says he doesn't know which one was the more scared. By the time Dale got his .30-30 out of the house the bear was four miles off."

Burchard Bower had made up his mind to leave the north. He was missing the folks back home..."Be glad to get back to Detroit and all my friends again! I wouldn't have missed this experience for the world though and have learned more of actual life and a good many other things than I have in any three years at home and in college." Dale Roselle was bitten with the lure of the wilderness and would stay to make the river country his home. He continued to prospect and help run a trading posts and, in fact, became an excellent riverman.

The financial depression that was soon to follow and last throughout the decade of the 1930s brought even more gold seekers into the Finlay Forks area. The adventures of Burchard Bower and Dale Roselle were no doubt repeated in similar fashion by hundreds of adventurous miners over the next ten years.

A Trapper's Life

Leap back in time, if you will, to the year 1940. About six decades ago in time, but light years distant in lifestyle and livelihood; a young man, twenty-seven years old, works the rivers and trails for a meager living and keeps a diary of his activities. His name is James Van Somer.

Jim trapped Copper Creek, Pine Creek and the steep country east of Deserters Canyon on the Finlay River. This had been Ben Corke's trapline, but Corke was too debilitated from a wound received in the First World War to trap anymore. Good legs and lungs are a trapping job prerequisite. In early October the young bachelor began to get set up for his winter's work. He got Corke to show him some of the trail heads and he now had to locate the line cabins and restock them for the long months ahead.

On October 16th he writes of his first tough day. "Came up from Pine Creek to Summit cabin and the going wasn't so hot, lots of windfalls and brush and both Smoke [his dog] and I had a hell of a pack [a trapper typically carried back pack loads of forty pounds or more]. It was almost too much for Smoke - he was just all played out but he kept coming like a gallant soldier." October 17th would be even worse because of wet snow and "damn miserable" rain. Jim finally reached Copper Cabin and found it to be only six feet by eight feet. This forty-eight-square-foot living space was going to be a little cramped; to make matters worse, the nearest firewood had to be packed from half a mile away.

The next morning Jim was going to return to Ben Corke's Trading Post on the Finlay to buy supplies. The sound of rain on the roof all night meant it would be a wet trip. "Wow, did I get soaked! I got wetter today and stayed wet longer than I can ever remember doing before. It rained all night then turned to snow that loaded the bushes and it was more like swimming than walking. I came right through to Ben's without stopping, in seven

Trappers and rivermen pose for photo at Fort Ware, 1930s. Left to right, John Bergman, Ludwig Smaaslet, Ellis Stolberg, Sam Miller, Enis Towers, Fred Forestberg (man playing horse unknown).

hours. Was so cold I couldn't even smoke - had to run wherever I could. Hope I never run into any more days like this."

The next few weeks were spent dunning out [sweeping out] the various cabins, cleaning out the root cellars [usually located under the floor boards of each cabin to keep food from freezing] and cutting firewood. One particular trail to the "Fork's cabin" had not been used in many years and was difficult to follow. On November 3rd, Sunday, Jim writes, "This is the Sabbath but I didn't feel much like praying, cursing seemed to be more like the order of the day. I came to the cabin on the Fork and had quite a time slipping and stumbling along - snow falling down my neck etc., fell in a mud hole up to my hip...so was very happy to get here and get dried out and a feed under my belt."

Using the Copper Creek cabin as the "home cabin" Jim began to set out traplines between the small lakes, along the rivers and creeks and between each cabin. The falling snow was beginning to pile up by mid-November; snowshoes would soon be a necessity. In the evenings, the solitude was broken by the little battery-operated radio Jim had packed into the Copper Creek cabin. He could get some U.S. stations as well as CBC once in awhile. On November 5th he was listening to the U.S. election returns. "So far Roosevelt is leading but not much hope he gets in."

The CBC carried messages to remote areas at certain times and, even if a trapper was not expecting a message, he would listen in for something interesting about a neighbor. The long winter evenings were when the baking chores were done and some of the trappers became quite good at bread making, as well as making homemade candy. The modern-day chef with his microwave and electric ovens would have been in awe of the products turned out on the top of wood heaters using tin boxes for ovens.

Jim would need a lot of fish for baiting the traps, so nets had to be used under the ice. Some of the catch would also be used to feed the dogs. If a good dolly varden or rainbow trout were caught, it would be eaten by the trapper to supplement his meager stores. "Went up to the lake to see the fish nets. Had twenty-four, a good catch, so Smoky had a good meal tonight. Had one big dolly ate half of it for supper, sure was good."

By November 7th the temperature was dropping fast and the pine martens were beginning to move about. The month of November is the best time to trap these large members of the weasel family and Jim was beginning to have some luck with two big martens caught. That evening he writes, "...Packed twenty traps and the flour...down to Copper Creek, tough going slipping and sliding in the snow. Still cold and clear. Cut some wood and made some custard for supper, stretched the marten and put two big patches on my pant legs. Seems like I'm always patching them, this brush is so hard on them"

The Finlay River Valley is a snow belt area and by late November Jim writes, "Snow, snow, snow, it's coming down and piling up." While a little snow is welcome, when there is a lot day after day it means leg-weary work tramping out the trails. To complicate matters Jim would be trapping the high country where fifteen years earlier young Ivor Smaaslett had been buried by an avalanche. Each fresh snowfall meant the traps would be buried and would have to be dug out and reset each time. The snow was putting the marten catch well behind, and a good sense of humor was exhibited by Jim where he writes, "Tuesday November 26, 1940 Station S.N.O.W. now brings you the day's news for Copper Creek district covered by Snowshoe Press, James Van Somer and his dog Smoky, sole inhabitants of this remote region comprising hundreds of square miles. More snow is the chief

Slim Cowart and Jack Adams pole their small boat up a stream five miles from the Peace River, 1920s. *Photo: Don Adams*

cause of interest today folks and that combined with no marten is the chief cause of discontent."

A trapper's pride was at stake if he didn't get a decent catch on a good marten line, and by November 27th Jim was feeling a little down when he writes, "Failed again. Sum total of today's labor is one weasel [worth about $1]. Should have had a marten - one was right to a trap but the pole had fallen down and trap was sprung. One other trap was sprung [by the weight of the snow], anyhow it's damn tough luck. No other tracks so far but jumped one moose. I think I'll go back to the main creek and set some more traps and see if I can't find someplace where the marten are thicker. I can't keep this up, they [the marten] are coming too slow altogether and it will look bad if I don't make at least a fair catch this year."

By December 5th a total of 115 marten traps had been set and the work of snowshoeing around the many miles of trail to check this many traps was considerable. With the snow so deep the dog

Dick Corless with four black wolves shot near Crooked River, 1930s. A bounty of $50 was paid by the government of B.C. for every wolf killed. *Photo: Jack Corless*

Smoky could not even carry his light dog pack anymore. "I never saw snow come this way before; I can never seem to get a trail broke and my traps are always snowed up." The hard work was taking its toll on Jim and his hand was giving him trouble as well. He had injured it earlier in the season and it was slow to heal. "My hand is not so good either. It's swelling up more and hurts like hell sometimes. I had to get up last night and soak it in hot water, which seems to help it."

Trappers are eternal optimists, however, and one good day will erase the memory of the many poor ones. December 12, "...Well, well fancy that! I got a marten after all. Small but dark [dark skins brought the highest prices]. Would have had one more too but a whiskey jack [Canada jay] had been in the trap. Also saw a moose up near the Pass...Sure was beautiful day, clear and cold, some wonderful chances for pictures. It is the prettiest mountain pass I ever saw."

Beaver meat is the best bait there is for virtually all types of carnivorous furbearers but Van Somer was forced by law to not trap beaver until March. This is why he had to use fish for bait, a definite handicap. Jim knew this and writes, "I saw several marten tracks near the mouth of the Forks but none very close to traps, though this should have been close enough to smell the bait. I sure wish I had some different bait." On top of the bait sit-

158

uation another problem arose. The scourge of the trapline is the wolverine. "A wolverine is following my trail all over, I hope he doesn't get any fur on me."

Getting enough food to eat each day, what with the hard physical work, is important for both man and dogs. The meals are planned out well in advance as most of the staples have to be packed in and protein on the hoof is not easy to come by at certain times of the year. On December 20th it was noted, "I gave Smoke a damned good licking tonight. He stole the meat he was supposed to have for tomorrow after I'd fed him, so tomorrow he gets none." The next day was also a bad one for Jim. "A lousy day, lousy trapping, and I felt lousy. I went over Copper Pass and as usual got skunked and as usual saw marten tracks. One went right under a trap pole and another crossed the trail within a hundred feet of a trap, guess my bait is no good - wish I had some beaver castor [scent glands on a beaver]. Seems like one marten to a trip is the best I can do, which is very poor in what is supposed to be marten country."

Christmas time can be very lonely for a trapper. He is bound to think of family, friends, and perhaps a lover back home. All alone Christmas Eve Jim notes, "So this is Xmas Eve! Well, it's sure a white one here, the snow is piling up; looks like I'll have some real trail breaking for a Xmas present. I wonder if I hung my sock up I'd get a marten in it... Guess I'll go to bed and see what Santa brings me." Christmas Day was the first Jim had spent alone, and except for a bigger than normal supper it was, to say the least, uneventful. On Boxing Day Jim's entry betrays a little sarcastic humor. "Well Xmas is over thank gosh, all the rush and bustle buying presents, visiting friends and gorging oneself on turkey, plum pudding, and so on gets a person down. Oh yeah, have some more beans Jim? Sure James, don't mind if I do."

Even a minor accident, when a man is alone in the cold climate, can be fatal. Just before New Years Jim cut his knee with his ax while out on the line. "I didn't think I would be able to make it all the way...my knee was pretty stiff and breaking trail up hill was pretty tough." He was planning a trip out to the trading post in four days time. "It's pretty stiff again to-night but I think I can manage all right on it...I can't travel very far and may not be able to keep warm if it gets real cold." On December 31st he is on the mend and his trapper's optimism is once again evident. "The end of 1940. Well I guess I can't kick on how I've made out [trapping]. I came down to my little cabin today and though my knee is sort of sore I can get along on it okay. I'm damn lucky it wasn't worse."

On January 3rd he left the trapline for a couple of weeks out at the trading post and Fort Grahame. He was looking forward to this outing, "...apple pie, eggs, etc. high tone grub, and also the mail. I should have a few letters by now and maybe a crock of rum." While at Fort Grahame he sold the nine marten pelts he had caught for an average of $35 each; $315 total for three months' work.

Jim acquired an extra dog from Corke for the rest of the winter. "Sandy is a good dog - [he] can pack more than Smoky." The animal would make it that much easier to get around but would necessitate more time getting fish for dog feed. Sandy helped out here as well, as he was adept at flushing grouse, so Jim could add

Residents of Finlay Forks, 1934. Left to right, George New, James Van Somer, Victor Williams, Lois Carlson, Andy Carlson.   *Photo: Jim Van Somer*

160

these to the pot. By late January the weather was cooperating as well, with very little snow although the temperature was dropping to -36°F every night. Jim was now packing a .30-30 "in hopes of seeing a moose." A slight chinook or warm spell came to the river country on the 29th of January. It brought out the ptarmigan as well as the marten, with Jim getting some of each. The rabbit snares were also producing results. On February 17th Jim records seeing both deer and cougar tracks. That wolverine was back and was robbing a few of the trap sets. By late February the lack of new snow made the traveling much better and Jim says, "Sure is wonderful going and looks like the weather will hold for awhile yet. It's -24F now and clear as can be...Hi Ho it's not such a bad life after all."

By mid-March the marten catch was definitely on the upswing, "Whoopie! picked up three marten today...a full and successful day. " The afternoon of March 17th found Jim skinning out two more marten and three weasels, "Cooked a pot of beans and ate bread and so another day passes, St. Patricks Day if I'm not mistook." March 18th was a mild day with the temperature above freezing and Jim having to cut snow and ice away from in front of his cabin. "This damn place is in a hole and all the water runs in through the door. Have quite a swimming hole in here."

With the dog food supply down, Jim had to spend more and more time fishing. March 22nd was a lucky day on this front. Using a hand line through a hole in the ice he pulled nineteen fish out "as fast as I could put the hook in, seventeen dollies [dolly varden] and two rainbow."

Jim Van Somer finished the trapping season off by trapping for spring beaver and was off for civilization and a little high life by the first of April, 1941. He would be back after the river freighting season was over to trap the following winter and for many years afterward.

Men of the Cloth

Right on the heels of the great explorers and fur traders came the missionaries—Catholic and Anglican for the most part. Not long after Simon Fraser and Alexander Mackenzie passed through northern B.C., the Roman Catholic Church established itself at Fort McLeod. The British-based fur companies enforced their ideas of civil law and order on the Native Indians and the church attempted to introduce the moral laws of Christianity. The fur traders themselves were not necessarily particularly religious, but they encouraged the missionaries to come, and it didn't matter what denomination they were. The Hudson's Bay Company wanted a steady supply of fur and Indian tribes that were warring with one another were not out trapping animals. Christianity seemed to bring a measure of stability to the Indians' lives.

Of course, in return for the hospitality of the Hudson's Bay Company, the priest or pastor was encouraged to pass the word to his parishioners that they should do their trading at the Bay post. The Catholic missionaries to the Indians of the river country were of the order OMI (Oblates of Mary Immaculate). These priests and nuns were very successful with the conversion of the Carrier Sekani people. The church influence can be seen even today with almost all the reserves sporting a church building. In 1842 the first Catholic priest, Fr. Modeste Demeres, arrived in Fort George. He found many of the French Canadians and fur traders living with Indian women and "he regularized their unions." Fr. Lejac opened a church on Stuart Lake in 1869 and this building, Chapel of St. Paul, was still standing in 1950. Fr. Lejac and Fr. McGuckin both worked the river country and performed baptisms at McLeod Lake in the 1870s.

Father A. G. Morice was the most famous of the Oblate priests to minister to the Natives. He was stationed at Fort St. James but was at heart an explorer and linguist and traveled extensively. On one of his longer forays he boated north from

Fort St. James by canoe, crossing the length of Stuart, Trembler and Takla Lakes. The priest and his Carrier guides carried on upstream on the mosquito-infested Driftwood River to eventually arrive at Bear Lake. The toughest part of the journey was still to come—the overland trek to Fort Graham on the Finlay River. Their route required the climbing of several mountains, and the valleys they crossed were choked with blowdown. The adventurers were glad to be back on water again at Fort Graham. After spending a few days at Fort Graham and Finlay Forks, the party traveled down to McLeod Lake. A welcoming party greeted the travelers and a feast was prepared that included, "caribou tongue and moose snout." This round trip from Fort St. James and back took five weeks.

Father Morice received an annual fee (some would call it a bribe) of $50 from the Hudson's Bay Company. This was paid to the priest for him to encourage the locals to sell their furs to the local Bay post. As a further incentive, the priest received his mail delivery from Fort George free of charge. This is not to say relations were perfect between the Catholic missionaries and the Hudson's Bay Company. Father Morice believed the Company was too paternalistic to the Natives, but he did recognize the Bay's genuine help for the destitute and elderly Indians and commended their refusal to stock or sell liquor in the Bay posts. Father Morice credited his church with bettering the lot of the Indian women. Before the missionaries came, Morice claimed, "The Carrier woman was not the queen of the home as with us [whites], but a servant, a drudge, and a slave."

The year of 1924 was a memorable one for the Christians of the Rocky Mountain Trench when the bishop visited all the settlements. Bishop Emile-Marie Bunoz was definitely not a desk jockey. Over his long career he managed to visit all the frontier parishes in his prefecture. His area covered the entire northern half of British Columbia and north into the Yukon Territory.

The north was virtually inaccessible by road when Bunoz became bishop in 1917. This wilderness was a far cry from his native France and he had to use horses, steamboat, riverboat and dog team to reach the frontier posts. During his eight years as a priest serving the Klondike gold miners he stated he felt he had slept on the ground for nine years. Missionaries, by necessity, often acted as doctors. Bunoz had witnessed the ravages of tuberculosis affecting the Natives especially, and had lived through the great influenza epidemic of 1918 where whole families, white and Indian, had died.

On June 27, 1924, Pierre Roy and George Roy, using their riverboat powered by the earliest two-horsepower outboard, started down the Crooked River with Bishop Bunoz and another priest aboard. In his diary it is clear he appreciated the wild river country, "...a beautiful river easy to navigate, lots of rich flat land, far off spruce and poplars," and along the bends itself, "...immense colonnades of willows, alders leaning on the waters, few birches, gigantic ferns, wild roses abound and diffuse a delightful aroma on the breeze, a variety of views." The bishop insisted on stopping to talk to all the trappers and miners they encountered en route. On June 28th they arrived late in the day at Finlay Forks and stayed at the Forestry House located there as a guest of Mr. McCleod the forester. The next day being Sunday, a service was held in the house.

June 30th found the party working their way up against the flow of the powerful Finlay River. His Excellency was right in the water with the others, pulling on the ropes and working with the poles to help the underpowered boat along.

Eventually they reached Fort Graham and a small welcoming committee was on the bank waiting for them. The manager of the Hudson's Bay Company offered his warehouse for use as a church and preparations were made for the service. The altar was made of packing cases with a bear skin thrown over the top. The manager supplied a white linen cloth to put on top of the bear rug and the assembly sat on bales of fur. Bishop Bunoz called it the "Church of Nature." Indians from as far away as White River (Fort Ware), about ninety miles away, were in attendance at this first historical mass by a bishop. One old patriarch from White River had met Father Lejac, but most of the Natives had never seen a priest, let alone a bishop, before.

The day after his arrival at Fort Graham the bishop performed a mere thirty-seven baptisms, fifty-two confirmations and ten marriages! Some of the marriages were a little tricky. Polygamy was common among the Natives, and if a man had three wives he was instructed to pick out one only for a proper marriage and to dismiss the others. Needless to say the two women that were dumped were not impressed.

Bishop Bunoz left a big impression on the locals and they promised they would build him a church if he came back for another visit. He did.

Seven years after that first visit Bishop Bunoz again found himself on the Crooked River headed north. It was 1931, in the midst of the great Depression, and Sub Chief Edward of McLeod Lake was engaged to bring Bunoz to visit his river parish. Chief Edward had his entire family of nine along and the good bishop had to find a spot for himself on the crowded boat. Bunoz says of the windy Crooked River, "The name is no misnomer - the river is real crooked and real rocky. We watched a bear eating a rotten moose on shore." The Edward family was living off the land and they fished and hunted as they traveled. On the Parsnip River the Bishop states, "I helped skin out a baby moose."

One June 23rd a stop was made on the shore of the Finlay to baptize two men; no doubt there was no shortage of water for this job. When Fort Graham was sighted, the first thing Bishop Bunoz noticed was the new log church that had been built. The news of his coming had spread and more than seventy people were on hand to welcome him. The bishop states of the little church, "It was very modest indeed, log walls and three windows - a small cross on the front and a rough altar." Bunoz found the Indians and white trappers shared much the same problems, "Game scarce, Depression fur prices too low, and costs of goods high due to freight costs."

After a few days attending church duties, the bishop and the Edward family headed south for Summit Lake. On Crooked River, the party was caught in a fierce thunderstorm, not uncommon in that country, and Edward pulled into the "Russian place" as the Natives called the home of Louis and Marie Tereshuk. No one was at home so the Natives just made themselves comfortable in the kitchen. The bishop felt uneasy about this taking over of someone else's house. Soon a canoe appeared with Marie and three children aboard. The bishop began to apologize, but Marie said of the Indians, "They did well," and she invited the bishop into the sitting room for a visit. Mrs. Tereshuk invited all to spend the night, but as there were fifteen in the party they decided to camp out a little farther upstream instead. That night the bishop had a pack rat walk over him as he slept and discovered some of his belongings had been chewed on during the night. That morning one of Sub Chief Edward's sons cut himself with an ax and the bishop was pressed into service to sew the young man up.

Bishop Bunoz took minor problems like this in his stride but had to face a few major tragedies as well. Usually the Bishop traveled with another priest for these infrequent visits. On a number of occasions a Fr. Elphege Allard accompanied him. Fr. Allard was a seasoned riverman of thirteen years' experience on northern rivers and the bishop felt at ease with Allard at the controls. Alas, tragedy struck in July, 1935, as the two priests were traveling down the Eagle (Dease) River of northern B.C.

The bishop was bowman with Allard running the kicker when they were attempting to negotiate the Cottonwood Rapids. As they passed under an overhanging limb Bunoz ducked and the tree swept some freight boxes off the top of the loaded boat. Looking back, he saw his bed roll and other effects floating in the river, and noticed that Fr. Allard had disappeared. "Stunned, I tried to stop the boat [with his pole], but the

water was so swift and the motor still running...I thought I saw Fr. Allard coming on the surface and going down almost immediately, the current was too much for any man." After being stranded on the lonely shore for about twenty-four hours Bishop Bunoz attracted the attention of a freighter going upstream in his boat. The freighter loaned the bishop two of his men and the journey was continued down to McDame Creek where the tragedy was reported to the provincial police.

Bishop Bunoz was a trail blazer for the missionaries to follow and left a favorable impression on all the rivermen, Christian and non-Christian alike, during his visits to the river country.

The old church at McLeod Lake was in bad shape and a decision was made to build a new one on the opposite side of the lake. Fr. Gerard Clenaghan was the pastor to the river communities from 1947 to 1966. He was also a carpenter and had the calloused hands of a man not afraid of work. He was at the sod breaking and worked until the completion of the new church in 1958. There was no power, and a portable light plant was used for working late into the evening. The new church had pews; in the old one, the worshipers had to sit on the floor. The church was completed in time for Christmas Eve mass.

A lay worker named Frank Roberts kept a journal of the event and wrote, "The first arrivals were three old Indian ladies - Annie, Betsy and Nellie, who had crossed McLeod Lake on the ice...the three ancients were followed by a steady trickle of

Fr. Clenaghan performing a Sunday service on the banks of the Pack River, 1959.
Photo: Prince George Catholic Church Diocese

natives and by a number of white families...even the Hudson's Bay Company store keeper came, a staunch Presbyterian."

Hymns were sung in English followed by a long hymn in the Carrier tongue. When the service was over it was discovered that the three old ladies were too played out to re-cross the lake, so a dog sled was produced but no dogs were available. Several teenagers were pressed into service. "These lads, playful devils, had somewhere acquired a quantity of fire crackers and the last we saw of this part of the congregation was blurred in flying snow as the sled took off across the lake at high speed with fire crackers bursting like machine-gun fire, the young men laughing heartily and the old women holding on for dear life. This was Christmas at McLeod Lake 1958."

Fr. Clenaghan was no stranger to water and was right at home on a riverboat. In 1959 using a forty-four-foot boat borrowed from Art Van Somer, Fr. Clenaghan and Frank Roberts set off for Ingenika. Also along was a trapper named Art Gagnon using his own thirty-two-footer. Both craft were loaded down with construction supplies including a portable sawmill. The three men were going to build another church at Ingenika!

Gagnon had been asked to supply the food and as such was in charge of cooking. Meals consisted of beaver and bear meat and when the party tired of that there was bear and beaver meat. When an Indian encampment was found, Fr. Clenaghan would insist on stopping for a visit and usually a service would be held. Two or three poles lashed between two trees would be the altar and logs would be used for seats. The day before the three men arrived at Ingenika, Art Gagnon shot a moose on the river; the first job when they arrived was to divide up the meat for the locals and building crew.

The church was to be made out of logs squared on two sides but a problem arose; there were no means to haul the timbers from the logging site to the church site. The Sekani Indians soon had a "wagon" made up. The entire rig was made of wood, including the axles. For wheels, the men cut the ends off logs. And with these wooden wheels and a long pine pole for a tongue, raw manpower got the logs moved.

The Sekani Indians of Ingenika built this wagon for work on the new church, 1959.
Photo: Frank Roberts and Prince George Catholic Church Diocese

June 7, 1959, was a big day. The construction project was completed in only two and a half weeks, and a service was held in the new St. Josephs, followed by a baptism. The portable power plant Fr. Clenaghan had brought along was fired up, and, using a projector he had brought, the church now became a movie theater. The movie presented? "A rip roaring western, Texas Kid."

It was now time for the two clerics and Gagnon to leave Ingenika and head further north for Fort Ware. At the fearsome rapids in Deserters Canyon trouble began. The three men had left the smaller riverboat at Ingenika, and with only the heavily loaded forty-four footer, their twenty-five horsepower motor was not powerful enough. After a few frightening tries at the canyon Roberts wrote, "we were forced to retreat...Fr. Clenaghan celebrated [prayed] the Eucharist but still we didn't make it." About this time the frustrated clerics heard an outboard motor and who should come into sight but Art Van Somer piloting his big boat. "Art agreed to carry our load through the canyon with his similar but higher powered boat...we experienced no further difficul-

169

ty...He's a real pro who started on the Finlay in 1924." Sometimes God really does provide.

When the tired men finally reached Fort Ware a welcome rest was in order. Such was not to be. The building project at Ingenika was to be repeated and a church was built at Fort Ware—God's work is never done.

The pioneer missionaries left their mark on the North. They were often relied upon for emergency medical service in the absence of any doctors. This sometimes included acting as a midwife. The churches they manned were often a safe haven for people in abusive situations. The missionaries' mere presence encouraged the traders to treat the trappers in a fair manner. The small rustic churches these men of the cloth built can still be seen today in the small communities across the North.

The End of an Era

When the Alaska Highway was built with its southern terminus at Dawson Creek, B.C., plans for a road connection from Prince George were soon discussed. The road north from Prince George was the Old Summit Lake Road. This was a rough, gravel road with some difficult sections, particularly where the road wound up the Salmon River hill. It had been the only road for the river freight since after the first World War.

The contract was let to build the John Hart Highway from Prince George to Dawson Creek and work began just after World War II. The road construction crews had built the road past Davie Lake by 1949, and the hardest section of Crooked River could now be bypassed by trucking the supplies to McLeod Lake. This made life a lot easier for the trappers and river freighters. Eventually the Parsnip River was bridged and then the trappers who made their living along the Upper Parsnip could truck their supplies to the river and load their boats. The hunting guides who operated up north in the Finlay country would also pick up their clients at the new bridge crossing.

The Parsnip River Bridge continued to be the southern terminus for the rivermen for the next twenty years and, except for improvements to the outboard engines, the river freighting business remained much as it always did. In the late 1960s a rough road was built from just north of the Parsnip River bridge up to Finlay Forks. This road was used to get access to the timber that grew along the Parsnip River valley.

The feasibility of harnessing the hydroelectric potential of the Rocky Mountain Trench began to be investigated seriously in the 1950s by the provincial government. The German industrialist Dr. Wenner-Gren and his associate Elmer Nelson were interested in tapping the resources of the Omineca and Peace country. Nelson knew the Pacific Great Eastern Railway would eventually extend farther northward to Dawson Creek and he lobbied for

Some of the homes at Finaly Forks, 1967—a ghost town awaiting the flood.

Photo: Joan Curtin

the rail line to be run up the trench of the Rockies. Both men had in mind to develop hydro power and build lumber and pulp mills. They envisioned a monorail being built, a relatively new rail concept at that time, to carry passengers and supplies up the trench. Their plans were not to be.

In 1963 the provincial government of British Columbia called for bids to build one of the largest earthen dams in the world. It would be constructed at the Peace Canyon and would be 600 feet high. Negotiations were begun to compensate some of the trappers and settlers who would be affected by the huge reservoir that would be formed. The larger traplines were bought out for a few thousand dollars, a paltry sum considering the many cabins that had been built on each line (they were usually spaced every six to ten miles apart). Miles of trail had been cut out laboriously by hand, and boats had been built and stationed on the lakes of each line by the trappers. The buy-out was essentially a take it or leave it deal. The province had hired Alf Janks and later Gord McMullen to burn every cabin down, and they would receive money for every cabin burned. A photo of the burning cabin was proof of the job completed. Janks attempted to burn some cabins two or three years in advance of the flood waters. Needless to say he was not well received by those who were still using them. On one occasion he was run off at gun point.

172

The spring of 1968 was a time of infamy for the rivermen. The gates to the three diversion tunnels were closed and the mighty Peace River was stopped by the WAC Bennett Dam. With the spring runoff at its peak, the reservoir began to rise rapidly, catching many off guard.

One trapper tied his boat up to a tree on the riverbank and settled into his cabin for the night. Imagine his surprise when he rolled out of bed the next morning to step into two inches of water. He hurriedly dressed and went outside to see his riverboat floating out of reach with the bow almost under water. It was lucky he had tied the bow rope with a fair amount of slack. He managed to use a pole to swing the stern around within reach and once on board he had to cut the bow line to free the boat. He then motored downstream on the Finlay to see if any ice jam had formed causing the river to back up. Soon others, including some Sekani Natives from Finlay Forks, were on the river to see what was the matter. No ice jam was found. The waters of the now-dammed Peace River were rising much faster than was originally forecast. Along the narrow reach of the Peace River, the water rose ten feet a night.

The human population was not the only thing affected; wildlife was caught off-guard too. As the wide valley around Finlay Forks began to flood, hundreds of moose, bears and other wildlife became stranded on islands that were formed by the rising water. Trees, logs and other floating debris prevented the animals from swimming to shore and hundreds of moose drowned.

Pen Powel, a bush pilot from Hudson Hope, flew his small plane over Finlay Forks in the fall of 1968. Near the mouth of the Omineca there was a hill that rose above the surrounding country. The slashing crews had cut the big spruce and pine trees on this promontory and the logs lay like pick-up sticks. This hill now became an island as the waters rose and it was to this high point the moose gathered to try and find refuge. The moose now became trapped as they could not leave due to floating debris. Powell returned a week later and counted more than 100 dead moose on the flooded island. Of course, more than just moose died; Powell said, "Even animals you don't often see in the water were swimming for their lives—weasels, mice, even squirrels. The squirrels would swim with their tail straight up out of the water." By late summer of 1969 the smell of rotting moose carcasses was everywhere. The floating animals had bloated and were caught in the debris piles. For the next two years the moose would try to cross the river as they always had and would exhaust themselves trying to swim around and through the logs that were piling up in the shallows of the forming lake. By 1972 the entire north end of Williston Lake was choked with logs and even the tug boats could not get through.

The flood waters eventually stretched from the Peace Canyon on the east, north to Deserters Canyon on the Finlay and south to almost where the Hart Highway crosses the Parsnip. The historic rapids of Deserters Canyon were now tamed, flooded under fifteen feet of water; also, gone forever were the Ne Perle Pas and Finlay Rapids on the Peace. The Omineca River was flooded ten miles up past the Black Canyon. The lower reaches of the Ospika and Ingenika Rivers were also lost. Old Fort Graham became only a memory and Finlay Forks rests under 300 feet of water.

Some of the old rivermen tried to carry on in the early years as Williston Lake rose, but the old flat-bottomed riverboats were no match for the big waves encountered on the wind-blown lake. On one occasion Art Van Somer was attempting to leave for Fort Ware with a big load of freight on board his forty-four-footer. As he pulled out of a cove protected from the wind near Finlay Forks, he encountered five-foot waves on the main lake and swamped his boat. His brother Jim rescued him and his overturned boat using a small tug boat, but more than $2,000 worth of supplies were lost. The hunting guide Ken Christopher left Fort Graham for Finlay Forks for a trip that would normally take hours; instead it took two days of hard work pushing and pulling his boat around the floating debris. He had on board two injured tree fallers who needed emergency treatment in Prince George. Eventually a tug boat had to be called and it plowed out a channel for the log-jammed riverboat to follow.

The Indians near Finlay Forks kept moving their camp to higher ground every few days. They did not understand the situation and figured the flood would eventually stop; it did, but not until a huge inland sea that was twenty miles across had formed. Their communities at Fort Graham and Ingenika were completely drowned out. The Native graveyard at Fort Graham was located on a high bank, and as the waters rose the bank sloughed in. The wooden caskets could be seen sliding down into the forming lake. Ed Stranberg was the last resident of Finlay Forks to pull out, surrendering his cabin to the flood waters.

When I was on the lake in its early years (1973), boating was very dangerous because of half-submerged deadheads. When the afternoon wind came up, the waves formed would force me into shore, if a passage could be found through the flotsam of logs. Submerged trees would let go from the lake bottom and rocket to the surface like torpedoes. A lot of sloughing in has occurred on the surrounding hill sides as unstable ground was flooded.

By 1990, however, the lake's condition had improved considerably. B.C. Hydro and various logging companies worked for years cleaning up the logs and the majority of the remainder had become water logged and sank to the bottom. It is now possible to reach the beach in most places. The moose and other wildlife eventually adapted to the big lake and, in fact, the fishing is excellent for dolly varden especially where the creeks enter.

I went on a tour of the powerhouse and dam in 1978 with my family. It is without a doubt an impressive marvel of engineering. But as I stood on the viewing site overlooking the dam and the flooded valley behind it, a feeling of sadness came over me. The era of the rivermen was over.

References

Don Gilliland of Germanson Landing: His Life Story, as revised by Margaret Owen (Self published by Don Gilliland and Margaret Owen, Feb. 1996).

Finlay's River, by R. M. Patterson (Toronto: MacMillan of Canada, 1968).

Peace River Chronicles, by Gordon F. Bowes (Prescott Pub. Co., 1963).

Notebook on the Peace River, by Jim Gould (Self published, 1979).

The Peace Makers, by Edith Kyllo (Self published, 1973).

Will to Power: The Missionary Career of Father Morice, by David Mulhall (UBC Press, 1986).

The Sikhani Indians of Fort Graham on the Finlay River in Northern B.C., by John Revel (NS Publishers, 1983).